Listen Learn Lead

Courage to Ask Power to Save

KENNETH KOON

ISBN: 198512369X
ISBN-13: 978-1985123694

DEDICATION

To all who fight to save lives on
the battlefield of personal despair.

FOREWORD

Listen Learn Lead is a work with tremendous capacity to give readers the power and skills to save lives. Chaplain Kenneth Koon offers a concise framework that individuals from all walks of life can utilize to intervene for those in need. The skills learned will enable the reader to lead those overwhelmed with thoughts of suicide to a safe place. Ken's first-hand experience intervening with those at risk will benefit all people. I have worked with him. I have seen his power of warmth and his capacity for empathy. He truly connects with everyone he touches. When we have worked together and taught others the skills on intervening in suicidal risk, his ability to connect and truly engage is masterful. I have great admiration for his talents.

Listen Learn Lead is his testimony of how one man has learned to connect with others and what he offers the reader are the skills to hear a person's message of despair, help them to find reasons for living, and lead them out of the darkness. Chaplain Koon is a proven and compassionate leader and Master Trainer in various intervention models. Notwithstanding this expertise, he has now catapulted his desire to eradicate suicide to new levels by offering this accumulation of his many experiences to thousands that he will never meet or personally train in one of his workshops. The reader will gain a vision of how to intuitively connect with those in despair and ask the tough questions of suicide.

Whether you are a family member of someone who is struggling with despair or various forms of melancholy, a first responder, minister, teacher, medical professional, or a crisis intervention specialist you will be well served by developing the skills offered in this book. The skills here will significantly enhance your ability to identify those in need, connect on a compassionate level, and save lives. You will be well-served to read and reread *Listen Learn Lead* so you are best prepared to engage when the need arises.

All of us can better prepare ourselves to be the one person who has the knowledge to make a difference for those in need. By following Ken's proven template of suicide intervention, the reader will be prepared to help those who may be contemplating suicide.

Paul D. Wade, PsyD, MS, LPC
Former Suicide Prevention Program Manager
99th Regional Support Command
U.S. Army Reserve, Ft Dix, NJ

LISTEN LEARN LEAD

CONTENTS

ACKNOWLEDGMENTS

First, I wish to acknowledge those I cannot call by name; the ones that now know that *Listen Learn Lead* is a model that saves lives, because it saved their life. Clearly 90% of the nearly 800 suicide interventions that I have conducted as of the writing of this book where instigated by a caring person that was concerned for a love one or friend. By be willing to engage their friends, the door was opened to those going through difficulty to find hope. Thank you for being an alert and caring person.

Much thanks to the 10,000 individuals that have participated in our workshops across the country to gain the skills that save lives. You have shared with me many miraculous stories of how the training saved a life, often within days of a workshop. You are the network of care that makes it possible to build a culture of community health.

To the many individuals, families, churches, civic organizations, and Foundations that have supported the mission of saving lives, YOU made it possible for me to be there for those at risk. You are the reason that many are alive today that thought they could not go another day. You are the reason that I was able to write *Listen Learn Lead*.

Jeanne Bowers, your calls when I have felt totally depleted after a difficult intervention have meant the world to me. Jeanne along with Cyndi Gall and their Equine Therapy program have helped restore my own sense of balance that has strengthened me to press on.

Tremendous thanks to Nancy Wayte, and others for proofing the book for me. Mrs. Wayte is my all-time favorite teacher, giving me a love for writing in the sixth grade. Her love for her students is one of my fondest memories.

These relationships above and so many others would not be possible without the relationship that I have with my family. My wife, Sherry is a lifesaver in her own right, working with those at risk. She is also a faithful companion, that prays for me daily in the work that I do. Her prayers have moved mountains. My youngest son, Tyler is probably also the youngest person that would know how to do a suicide intervention. For three years as a teen he ran the AV for our workshops. He could probably teach the workshop. Nathan and Chad have been a tremendous encouragement during our annual Courageous Challenge, a Saturday morning event involving hundreds of participants and volunteers in knocking out more than 25,000 push-ups to raise awareness and funds for the mission. Many other extended family members have been wonderful supporters of the work through their financial and emotional support and prayers. Finally, there is my oldest son, MaCrae. Were it not for his intervention in my own life I would not be here. He is the one that asked, "Dad are you thinking of suicide." He is the one that drove two and a half hours from Charleston Air Force Base to Ft Jackson at four in the morning to run PT with me and my unit. He restored my hope. Family is precious beyond words to me. The most notable achievement of my life is any part I might have played in building a strong family that loves and respects others.

KENNETH KOON

AUTHOR'S NOTE

I have written this book for the primary purpose of reaching those that want to know how they can save a life. I simply share with you, lessons learned from my personal experience in working with those that have been at risk and found a way to choose life. I have also written to validate the emotions such as anger that many survivors experience because they feel that more is not being done to address this epidemic. There is a suicide in the US every 12 minutes, and worldwide two suicides every minute, yet as Gregg Zoroya, wrote in USA TODAY, "America Simply Shrugs". But you have heard the alarm and you are ready to *do something now.* You may be angry; good! It's a starting point and much to be preferred to apathy. Let's just be sure to channel our anger in the right direction.

You may be a parent wanting to know how to help your child at risk or the adult child concerned about a parent. You may be a school teacher, a First Responder, or a nurse. You may be a current military member, a veteran, or a civilian. But you have someone in your life right now that you want to help. Those that are at risk are not the channel through which we express our anger. They are the ones that need our love, empathy, and understanding. There is a place for controlled anger in society, but anger is not called for from the one that is seeking to help the person at risk of suicide.

Peripherally, this book is also for every legislator that has the power to introduce bills that will strengthen the mental fiber of our nation for our veterans and the one million other Americans that attempt suicide each year. This book is for the Grant makers who have the ability to write grants for training that will equip thousands, instill courage, and restore hope.

Recently, our organization received a rejection letter from a large Medical Foundation. The line that I found most interesting in their response, "Our Board of Trustees desires to see funds used most expeditiously in meeting immediate health care needs." So, in their opinion, a person who is about to die is not an "immediate health care need." Sadly, once again mental health and suicide prevention specifically has been relegated to the chambers as the ugly step child.

This book is for pastors and the flock you tend. I was a pastor at one time. I went to seminary for my Master of Divinity degree and a few years later earned a Doctorate in Counseling. But it was not my formal education that prepared me for the work of suicide intervention; it was the US ARMY. Neither degree in those five years of education ever mentioned the word suicide. Many pastors have called me late at night unsure how to respond to the person at risk. They have shared with me that they feel ill equipped in this regard. Hopefully, we can connect at some point just as many other churches have done to host a *Listen Learn Lead* workshop.

Finally, this book is for the one that has already experienced loss. As the lead for our communities LOSS Team – Local Outreach to Suicide Survivors and in my work with more than 25,000 soldiers I have met many that grieve loss by suicide. I too have experienced such grief. There are many sleepless nights, unanswerable questions, feelings of guilt and anger. One phrase you will never hear from me is "I understand" for though I have experienced loss, I have not experienced your loss. What I do hope to convey to you is hope. Things will never be the same, but in our *new normal*, we can find hope.

Working through the book you will find in Part One the model of suicide intervention after which this book is entitled. *Listen Learn Lead* did not begin as a model for suicide intervention. I originally wrote the curriculum in 2013 as a model to address Toxic Leadership in Military Units. After further reflection I realized that with a few adjustments the model had efficacy for my work in suicide intervention, not just with Veterans, but for all people. In chapter two we will discover the incredible power of a simple question that moves us into the learning phase. We will look at why it is that many people struggle to ask the question that my son asked me. We will also dispel the myths that surround the question. Most importantly you will gain the courage and skill to ask the question yourself when you see the signs in a person at risk.

In Part Two I will simply share a few personal reflections of things I have learned along the way. I will also address the law enforcement community as well as the faith community sharing how my work in suicide intervention has honed my faith and how faith has transformed my understanding of suicide. Additionally, I hope to rally all communities to greater involvement on the battlefield. A survey by Lifeway Research recently revealed that, "Only 4 percent of churchgoers who have lost a close friend or family member to suicide say church leaders were aware of their loved one's struggles." Many church going people that I have provided postvention pastoral care for have shared that after loss they stopped attending church completely or moved to another church. One man said, "Every time I went to church I was reminded that my son was gone, because no one would speak his name. It was as if he never existed." As a person of faith, I know we can do better. The same occurs in the law enforcement community and the community as a whole; there is a loss that no one saw coming and we are unsure of the words to share when it does.

In my former career I was a real estate broker and educator. I love teaching and sold houses primarily to underwrite my love of teaching agents how to sell houses. I would take agents on educational cruises and never had problems selling seats in the classroom or rooms on a ship. When I transitioned to the work of suicide intervention it wasn't long before I was teaching others to do what I do; again, I love to teach. However, I thought I would fill classrooms teaching intervention in the same manner I did real estate. I thought I could save the world or at the very least my community. Such was not the case. Agents wanted to come to real estate classes to learn how to make more money. But let's be honest, who really wants to attend a suicide intervention class. Just as real estate agents attend real estate classes because that is what they do, individuals that attend suicide interventions workshops do so because of their personal familiarity with suicide. Most attendees have experienced loss of a friend or loved one. Many come looking for answers. The exception is the young soldier or the newly licensed counselor. The first is ordered to mandatory training that he would rather not be at and the latter is there because it can help in her job. But for everyone; it is a tough and often challenging day.

In chapter 17 we will look at the importance of self-care for the caregiver. I share from my own experience the importance of not trying to do this work alone. Care givers need care too. It is important to have a circle of friends that can support the cause. All are not called to do direct crisis intervention, some are called to support roles. The front line in battle is only as strong as the supply line. Care givers are notoriously bad at taking care of themselves, I know I was. But today, my circle has within it, individuals that are very good at reminding me to take care of myself. It's not a selfish act; it's vital to maintaining resilience of body, mind, and spirit. As one of my board members shared, "Ken you are on airplanes every month. What do they say? Put your own mask on first, before you attempt to help others." I'll share later the things that have helped me, and others maintain personal resilience.

In the appendix you will find a wide range of resources that can help you through the journey. *Listen Learn Lead* is not a substitute for medical or other professional care, but it can be a starting point.

Thank you for caring. It is highly likely that you are reading because you have someone in your life right now that is at risk or you have lost someone dear to you.

Rebecca, was a retired school teacher that lost her son to suicide. At first, she was hesitant to attend the workshop, but finally after several months she did. We now market *Listen Learn Lead* and all other workshops we teach under the banner of the *INTERVENE CHALLENGE*, because we know that it is a challenge for those that have experienced loss. It was a challenge for Rebecca the day she attended, but in a simulation exercise where she was the helper she had a break through. She wrote later, "The Challenge has given me a voice to help end the epidemic of suicide - one person at a time." Perhaps your story is like Rebecca's.

Thank you for your mindfulness to the circumstance of others. I often tell workshop attendees, "If you see the signs, the signs were meant for you." My law enforcement participants get it when I simulate being a police officer at the window of a person I have just pulled over, "Sir did you see that sign back there? It was meant for you."

What you should also know is that you will never feel fully adequate to the task. No one does, and if they do they will probably miss something, or they burn out within three years. We have trained hundreds of licensed therapist and First Responders who know the text book protocol for helping others, yet many call me when they find themselves facing the challenge personally; when it is no longer just a job, but it is their own parent or child. There have been many times after the question has been asked, when I too have struggled in the learning phase to help the person at risk find hope; when they are facing such incredible challenges in life.

While some find asking the question of suicide a challenge, the challenge for me is in those times when the person at risk is utterly broken in their hopelessness and I struggle to find anything meaningful that they might have to give them hope. If you haven't already discovered it, what you will find is there is a world around us filled with hurting people. Addressing the pain can be a challenge. But I suspect you already knew that since you have read this far. It's like when you buy a new car and suddenly it seems that everyone is driving the same model. Pain has a way of taking us out the bubble and into the real world. In that world we find people all around us dealing with incredibly overwhelming challenges; you may be one of them. My encouragement to you is to tell someone. Reach out to a caring counselor, pastor, or friend. Let your doctor know or call the national life line at 1-800-273-TALK.

Often, I will begin the *Listen Learn Lead* workshops with a quote from the preacher, Henry Ward Beecher, who wrote in 1863, "They hover as a cloud of witnesses over the nation." At the same time, I will present the Remembrance Wall; a collage of fifty faces of those that are no longer with us. I share briefly of their stories. I imagine that they are part of that great cloud of witnesses. The preacher spoke of those dying on the battlefield in the War Between the States; while I speak of those that have died on the battlefield of personal despair. I imagine them listening to see if someone will still mention their name.

There's 13-year-old Joey, he loved his family and the elderly ladies at church loved him as he would often help them to their cars. There's John the decorated Marine Cobra pilot who faithfully served his country. There's Kyle who was never hesitant to show kindness to those that were having a bad day. There's Stephanie who could give hope to others but could not find it for herself. Regardless of who I speak of, I always share the way they lived and loved life; it's never about how they died. Suicide is a tragedy, but it is their life I want to remember, not their death. If this cloud of witnesses could speak to us from across that great abyss I can imagine their words in a mighty chorus, "Take care of those that remain. Honor my memory by helping others find the hope I longed to know."

DO SOMETHING NOW

"If there is a God, do something now." These were the words a Marine veteran whispered all alone after his weapon misfired in an attempted suicide. The next moment his phone rang. I had called him at the request of a mutual friend that was concerned for his safety. In his darkest moment, help was on the way. Similar instances have happened in many of the more than 800 suicide interventions I have been involved in since founding Armed Forces Mission. Thousands of caregivers we have trained nationwide have also reported equally miraculous stories. Lives are being saved!

Sadly, I have also worked with many survivors; those that have lost loved ones to suicide. Some had prayed for a miracle knowing that a loved one or friend was at risk; while others were caught unaware saying, "we had no idea things were that bad." Unfortunately, when we consider that in the USA, 45,000 people a year die by suicide and 1 in 300 attempt suicides, we can't avoid the truth that things are bad.

There has been much discussion on how we should frame this crisis that plagues communities across the land. Some have suggested that we not use the word *epidemic*. In one sense they are right, suicide does not fit the generally accepted idea of a medical epidemic; it is after all not an infectious disease (or is it). There are no infecting bacteria that can be passed from one person to another simply because you were in the same room. On the other hand, according to the World Health Organization, a health crisis does not have to be contagious to be called an epidemic; such is the case with the obesity epidemic in America. In 2003 SARS (Severe acute respiratory syndrome) was classified as an epidemic. In that year, 774 deaths were reported in 37 countries. Suicide on the other hand takes more than one million lives a year worldwide.

We should always be careful with the words we use in the public domain. There is ample research to show that inappropriate public response can activate suicide clusters whether it be in a high school or a Combat unit. The same can be said of private conversations as well. Whenever, a person at risk is told they are *being silly* or they *just need to think positive thoughts* or *have more faith* it does not help the situation. Such response can escalate the risk when the crisis is not taken seriously, or the person at risk fails to have positive thoughts even though they try faithfully to do so.

Words are important. Recently a teen was found guilty of manslaughter for the words she texted to her boyfriend who then took his life. Yes, words are important, but it is equally important that we not deny the facts with the words that we use. If we don't use the word *epidemic* what word would be a better choice? Widespread, wave, prevalent, rampant, sweeping, skyrocketing, rash. If we fail to engage the public for fear of using the wrong words, we can be certain of one thing; the crisis will only get worse.

In my humble opinion, *epidemic* is a fitting word, particularly when we are conveying urgency to those that can and should be doing something to affect change. We can only build a culture of health where individual community members are safer from the risk of suicide by using the strongest words possible in addressing those that can make a difference. Words that don't wake a slumbering and complacent society are as useful as a smoke alarm with a dead battery in a house on fire. Weak words make weak culture. The piercing shrill of a loud alarm is never a welcome sound, but if the house is on fire we are grateful for the alarm that wakes us from sleep. If the house burns to the ground and even if no one was hurt, we wouldn't say it was just a small insignificant house fire; NO, it was a tragedy; photo albums gone, the love letters gone, the adorable little figurehead your child made in pottery class gone. Then the neighbor tries to console by saying, "I understand how you feel…why I remember just last summer our two-man pup tent was completely destroyed by fire on a camping trip…"

When the experts tell us not to use the word *epidemic*, we invalidate the pain and loss of hundreds and even thousands of grieving people that have used that very word in our workshops as they share their stories. I see anger increasing across our land along with the increase in suicide, because so few seem to understand the significance of loss that survivors feel.

In 2013, our first full year of service we saw a 50% reduction in the suicide rate from the previous year in my hometown community. In fact, it was the lowest rate in 20 years and half the national average. We were highly engaged that year in several interventions. We worked closely with law enforcement and everyone we worked with is still alive today. I was feeling good that we were moving the community in the position of strength. In the following year word was out about our workshops. I spent 70 to 80 percent of my time on the road in other communities or working with Soldiers in the Army Reserve. I shared our success in Washington DC at Military Intelligence Command Conferences and in Florida with the Army Medical Command. I spent several weeks in Jersey at Ft Dix training the largest force in the Regional Support Command. I was at Ft Dix on August 11, 2014 when I received dozens of text messages from friends wanting me to know that actor, Robin Williams had died. With much sweat and even a few tears we finally reached the 10,000 mark in the number of people that had participated in our workshops. I was leading the charge in training an army of soldiers and civilians to do what I do. My thought was if 10,000 workshop attendees will do even one percent of what I have done we will save 70,000 thousand lives.

By January of 2016, I was suffering from full blown compassion fatigue. The pace and the critical moments had caught up with me. My cortisol (the stress hormone) was constantly elevated 24 hours a day just in case I got the 3 am call. My cardiologist was expressing concern. I shared with another chaplain, "The nightmares of others have become my own nightmares." He said, "Ken, you sound like Captain Peter Linnerooth." "Who is that?", I asked. "I'm surprised you don't know. He was an Army psychologist; look him up." I spent the next hour reading and rereading the Captain's story in Stars and Stripes. I called his best friend that had been with him in battle. Linnerooth had counseled soldiers during some of the fiercest fighting in Iraq. Hundreds upon hundreds sought his help. He was described as one who could build instant rapport, show empathy, and change minds. He had a "big heart". But on Wednesday, January 2, 2013 this Bronze Star recipient ended his life. It was then I knew that something had to change. The vicarious trauma of working with hundreds of hurting people on the edge of life and death, along with my own Post Traumatic Stress had proven to me that I am no superman. I am just a man.

My initial thought was I will come off the road, I'll focus on my hometown again. Then I revisited the stats and discovered that our hometown suicide rate had tripled from where I left it and was now 20 percent higher than the national average. My heart sank. Like Linnerooth, I realized I couldn't fix a broken system; I couldn't save the world. I won't kill myself, I have been there; but I can't keep doing this…maybe I'll just go back in to real estate.

On January 13, 2016, another Wednesday, my wife, and I were headed to meet friends for dinner. They have been supporters of Armed Forces Mission since the founding day. Sherry had no idea about my plan to throw in the towel. I planned to tell our friends that they don't need to support the work anymore; I'm quitting. On the way to the restaurant Sherry kept saying, "Please don't talk about suicide, please, please don't talk about suicide." I didn't realize at the time that Sherry was also weary. She knew from experience that people either wanted to talk about what we do because they were in a crisis, or they avoided us because they mistakenly thought all we talked about was suicide. Sherry wanted to have a good evening simply visiting with friends; and with Greg and Gini we could do that, there was a balance of listening and sharing. Greg is in law enforcement and Gini is a nurse; we could laugh, have fun and be serious when the need called for it. As we stood in the lobby with Gini, Greg walked in and the first words he spoke, "That was a suicide!" "Where?" I responded. "Right there at the light in front of the restaurant." I didn't want this. I never want this, especially this night, but it seems to follow me wherever I go. I glanced at Sherry with an *I'm sorry* in my eyes and the phone rang; it was the police department. "We need you." - "I'm already there."

Army Veteran, Kyle Lovett had taken his life. After processing the scene, I was escorted to the parent's home. Three days later I did the memorial service. I never had the chance to admit defeat and I knew that night that I never could. Because even though I couldn't save Kyle only 75 yards from me, I knew there would always be another one that needs help. I also know now that the physical and emotional toll is a weight I cannot carry alone. But I will carry what I can. It is my hope that those who read this book would rise to the occasion, just as many others are. I suppose this is my greatest motivation for the book. If you choose to join me in the mission, I can tell you that there will always be another one that needs help. I should also tell you that we won't save the world but working together we can save someone's world. Who's with me?

In 1961, President Kennedy signed an executive order establishing the Peace Corps; their motto, "The Toughest Job You'll Ever Love." I've found mine; it's suicide intervention and training others to do the same. It's tough to be sure; especially in those times when it seems that nothing I do will stir the embers of hope under the ashes of despair. There have been many times I wanted to quit. But there is always one more. There was a day when I was that one. Had it not been for the love and compassion of one man, I would not be writing these words. That man was my oldest son, MaCrae.

A freak fire accident involving my third son, Chad was the culminating event in a series of tragedies that brought me to the edge of the proverbial bridge. Several other events had occurred in my life over a period of fifteen years which had chiseled away at my resilience, including being the first on scene at a massive tanker fire where I could not save the man whose car had careened into a fuel truck at a gas station. Those memories came flooding back when I heard the explosion that rattled the sunroom windows. I turned and saw 13-year-old, Chad running through the woods on fire. He had to be Air-Lifted to the Burn Center in Atlanta. The local Shriners got word of the accident from the cover story in our local newspaper and they sent us to their Children's Hospital in Cincinnati. The accident occurred on my watch, while Sherry was at the grocery store. I felt responsible; much like many of the soldiers I now counsel that have lost squad members. No one blamed me, but I blamed myself. Then the bills started coming in. While the Shriners Hospital did not cost us a penny, the helicopter ride to Atlanta was more than $20,000 and the Atlanta hospital bills were beyond my ability to pay. I had no medical insurance at the time, as I just stepped down from a position as pastor. The thought of suicide entered my mind.

Until the age of forty-five I had never had thoughts of suicide; some might even say I was unrealistically optimistic, a true Pollyanna. There was never a challenge too big that I couldn't conquer. I had experienced many difficulties in life, but I could always bounce back. So, I never told anyone of the very uncharacteristic thoughts that began to torment my mind. I have since learned that keeping those dark thoughts to myself was what gave the thoughts such power. In my own mind they seemed like such rational thoughts, but the moment I shared with my son, bringing the thoughts to light, those thoughts began to lose their power. My family had no idea that at night I would lay in bed reading the terms of a life insurance balance by the light of my cellphone. I never shared my thoughts with the Army recruiter as I signed the Age Waiver to go back into the military. It was my oldest son, MaCrae that I finally confided in. I did so because he asked a very simple question. "Dad are you having thoughts of suicide?"

I share *personal* stories to raise *personal* awareness, the awareness of individuals that are ready to do something now. There was a time in my superman days when I thought I could change the system and even the culture, but again, I am just a man. Those that I work with every day know the system is broken, at least in America.

We pass laws requiring teachers to receive mandatory training in intervention and by the time it gets to the actual teacher the training consist of a ten-minute YouTube presentation. In the summer of 2017, we trained more than 500 First Responders; these were not rookies, but seasoned veterans. Yet 95% had never had suicide intervention training prior to taking the *Listen Learn Lead* workshop. Multi-million-dollar Medical Foundations have gone on record sharing that they do not consider suicide to be "an immediate health care need." More than one veteran has ended his life in the parking lot of his local VA hospital, frustrated by a system that has let him down.

In the summer of 2017, Australia allocated $350 million dollars to address suicide among their veterans. In the US, our total budget for all people is one sixth that of Australia. By the way, the entire Australian military is half the size of the US Marine Corps. So, by the numbers, per person, our friends Down Under are allocating 27,000 percent more to suicide prevention than the US. The system is broken at least in the USA. But I am no longer inclined to concern myself with what our government is not doing, and one thing they're not doing is listening. I choose instead to invest my remaining kilowatts where someone is home and they are listening.

Regardless of what others may say, suicide *is* an *epidemic*; one that cuts a swath across every demographic. While certain segments have higher incidents, no segment has natural immunity. One segment that has received significant attention is the veteran population. There are many incredible organizations across the country seeking to raise awareness about the number of Veterans that take their lives each day; most are Veteran led, because we try to take care of our own, at least on a personal level. Many, like Armed Forces Mission and Stop Suicide USA, operate on a shoestring budget doing the best they can with what they have. It is my hope that we can network with one another in bringing the *Listen Learn Lead* workshop to those they serve.

While I can't change the culture, I can be one strand within the safety net of care working with others to make our communities safer for all people. Listening for and finding connections with other likeminded individuals and organizations is the true key to building a culture of mental health. I often wish that Superman or Wonder Woman would appear; I would be glad to support them in their efforts, but in my heart, I know that it is really teams that win championships. Even the champion boxer that gets all the glory and takes the title has a team that helped him get there. Winning the fight to eradicate suicide is an effort that will take many that are listening, learning, and leading.

If you do feel inadequate to the task, you will be glad to know that you are not the solution. Neither is this book the solution. This is not a book on how to solve every problem or restore someone to sound mental health. You won't earn a PhD from what I have to say. I speak in the language of ordinary people that are experiencing extraordinary circumstances. As Jill Hastings, PhD said after attending one of our workshops. "I appreciated the straight forward, realistic, "no psychobabble" approach in this workshop, and the focus on how as a community we can do something NOW to reduce suicides."

The Marine on a phone call needed something now and a PhD in the classroom said the same for her community. This is the purpose of the book; that anyone willing that takes the time to learn can do something now.

Listen Learn Lead is a first aid model, another tool for your first aid kit, like splints and bandages. Sometimes using the model will be enough and other times more intensive care will be needed. The day Chad was burned I did what I could do, but I also immediately called 911. Someone else flew the helicopter and another person administered the IV. What I am attempting to say is that you don't have to do this alone

As we listen we become aware of the signs all around us. When we ask the simple question, "Are you thinking of suicide?" we learn why the person at risk has come to this present state of mind. It is only through our ability to listen and our willingness to learn that we are then able to lead the person at risk to a place of safety. So, let's begin, because there will always be someone somewhere who is praying, "If there is a God do something now."

LISTEN

Nothing I say this day will teach me anything.
If I am going to learn, I must do it by listening.
Larry King

A dozen veterans were gathered around a large conference table for the inaugural meeting of the Board of Directors of Armed Forces Mission. They listened as I laid out the vision, much in the way that a Commander would share his intent in preparation for battle. In my mind it was a battle, one that was taking more than one hundred and fifteen American lives every day, a disproportional number being veterans. Within 15 minutes of our location there were 22,000 veterans, no doubt many of them contemplating suicide at that very moment. After I completed my presentation, one of the members asked, "What are we going to do when we complete the mission?" Granted, the typical military mindset is that we are given a mission, we deploy, achieve our desired end-state, and we come home. My response to the question was, "Sir, unfortunately it is my opinion that this will be a protracted engagement, a truly impossible mission. I don't see a time when Armed Forces Mission will ever transform into a bowling team or a bingo night." Thankfully, they got it. They understood the mission I asked them to join me in and we have been together now for five years fighting suicide. With their support I have been able to conduct 800 successful suicide interventions and train 10,000 others to do the same.

The Board members listened, and as they did, their awareness grew. They gained a better understanding of the battlefield and the resources that would be needed. They also saw what I and my team would need to be successful. In a similar way, if you are going to help someone that is at risk of suicide you must be willing to listen. Listening is the first step as we move into the *Listen Learn Lead* suicide intervention model, and it is more than the dictionary definition of simply trying to hear something. Marketing guru, Seth Godin, puts it best when he says, "You can listen to what people say, sure. But you will be far more effective if you listen to what people do." Listening involves a state of mindfulness where you are fully aware and fully present. You are listening with your whole being.

Listening answers, the *WHAT* question. Imagine it is Monday morning after the big upset at the Friday night high school football game. A defeated quarterback sits in your English class, despondently deliberating in his mind every missed opportunity. He blew it, and everyone knew it. He let the team down, and scouts from the University were there to see every embarrassing moment. What's going on? What's going on with your fellow sheriff's deputy headed home for the weekend to finally sign the divorce papers exactly sixty days after their three-month-old in his care died of Sudden Infant Death Syndrome while his wife was on a business trip. What's going on with the 65-year-old recently retired neighbor whose wife died of cancer and his children who live three states away never call to check on him? What's going on with your 12-year-old who is incessantly bullied at school, only to come home and sit alone in her room where the harassment continues through social media? A 2017 headline in the New York Post reads, "Former Facebook exec: Social media is 'ripping apart' society". In the 70s, when I was a child, home for most kids was a refuge for those that were bullied at school. Today that is not the case.

When you see what is going on it is time to engage in a caring conversation. As we truly listen, we hear things that others do not hear. We see what others do not see. In the words of music artist, Paul Simon, we see, "People talking without speaking" and the ones that show no signs at all may perhaps be at a greater risk than those that show signs. There are several reasons for this higher risk. If there are no signs, very few, if any, would be alerted to the risk. Some might say that the person that shows no signs is more serious about suicide than the one that is crying out through the signs they put off. One cannot know for sure; however there have been many instances when I was engaged in a suicide intervention with someone who showed no signs, and the risk was high, but they are still alive today.

Some may wonder how that last sentence is possible. If there are no signs, then why would you engage in an intervention? How would you know to do so? One workshop participant almost accusingly commented, "Well Ken, I guess you just ask everyone if they are suicidal?" No, the truth is I don't, but in theory I could, and every 20th person I asked would in fact be having thoughts of suicide and 1 in 300 will attempt in the next six months or already has attempted in the past six months. Signs are important, but it is not the primary thing I focus on, because sometimes, there are no signs. It may seem rather counterintuitive, but often I am quicker to jump into the question of suicide when there are no signs simply because in my own experience the risk is higher. But I haven't yet answered the question of how I knew.

Imagine the familiar four way stop that you must come to every day on your way to work. As you round the curve, you always see the large octagon with white letters on red background. You begin to slow down and come to a complete stop when it is your turn. Now imagine unbeknownst to you that the stop sign was wiped out by a cement truck. What do you do as you round the corner? If you have always relied on the sign, you may plow right through the four-way stop, and someone could be hurt. You were looking for a sign that wasn't there. The chances of injury are even higher for a driver unfamiliar with the area.

Situational Awareness

Half of Germany's Autobahn has no posted speed limits, yet their automobile casualty rate is $1/10^{th}$ that of the US. Situational awareness is far more important than any signs that a person at risk might exhibit. Answering the *what's going on* question is not so much about the interpretation of signs as it is an awareness of circumstances. The quarterback may not be despondent after the big loss. The widower may be actively engaged in a local civic organization, and the bullied teenager may continue to go about their regular activities with no signs whatsoever of the tremendous pain they feel inside. If we consider signs alone, we could easily miss that the person is suicidal. Then we wonder what happened when a tragedy does occur.

It is estimated that one in five teens will not present any signs of suicidal ideation. Several studies in both the US and the UK indicate that up to 50% of all suicides occur within minutes of making the decision to act. In many of those cases there were no signs. The reason I have engaged in so many interventions is because of circumstances, not signs. Anytime I become aware of changing circumstances in a person's life I engage in conversation. I don't immediately ask, "Are you thinking of suicide?" But I do want to check in on the person.

Think of signs as the things that people do that alert the helper to the risk. The risk then is the changing circumstances that the individual is facing. An elderly gentleman was diagnosed with an inoperable brain tumor. One of our workshop participants stopped by to check on him. As he talked it become evident to the helper that the man intended to end his life. She simply said in a calm tone of voice, "It sounds like you are thinking of suicide. Are you thinking of suicide?" From there she began to understand his why. He didn't want to be a burden on his family. He had seen others that lost their physical and mental faculties and he didn't want his family to have to deal with these things. He was a very proud man and the thought of losing control disturbed him immensely.

I tend to focus on circumstances more than signs, not only because sometimes there are no signs, but because signs can be deceptive. Signs may not be signs at all, but instead are part of the circumstances. My mother took our workshop and several weeks later she called me concerned about her sister. "She's giving things away, and you do know that she has had a mastectomy. I think she may be suicidal." I commended my mother for being alert and made a phone call to my aunt. We chatted for a few minutes and then had the following conversation:

Me: Mom asked me to give you a call because she was worried about you. She thought you might be having thoughts of suicide?

Aunt: Heavens no! Why would she think such a thing as that?

Me: She was concerned because of all you have been through with your health and then she heard that you were giving things away....

Aunt: I appreciate the concern, but I am not going to kill myself. I am giving the kids some things now, because I want to be able to enjoy giving things away while I am in my right state of mind to do so. I don't know what the future holds and giving my children things makes me happy.

Me: So, you're not suicidal?

Aunt: No, Kenneth, I am fine.

Me: I am glad to hear that. I love you....

While giving things away can be a sign of suicidal thought, in the case with my aunt it was not a sign of anything; it was part of the circumstances. Nevertheless, it was good to have that conversation for several reasons. First, it demonstrated care for another person. Secondly, it opened the door for future conversation should the thought of suicide ever present itself. What it did not do is put the thought of suicide in her mind, which we will discuss in a later chapter.

While I have participated in more than 800 suicide interventions, I have asked the question thousands of times; I am not always right about what I think I see. However, I have never had anyone slap me for asking or even seem to be offended by the question. Many workshop participants state that one of their greatest fears in asking is that they may be wrong. My response is always, "But what if you are right?" If the person is not suicidal they will typically respond by thanking the helper for demonstrating the concern that is evident because the helper was willing to ask. At the very least you have now identified yourself as a person that cares. Should the thought of suicide ever arise, the individual may seek you out for help. Several months after I had asked the suicide question of a soldier, he came to me saying, "You remember the discussion we had? I was suicidal then, but you didn't know me, and I didn't know you, so I said, 'No'. But others have told me of how you helped them. I would not have known had they not told me, so I know you maintain confidence. I needed help three months ago but was too afraid to say anything. Now the thoughts of suicide are stronger, and I know I need help."

Anything that a person does or does not do that is out of character with what they have done or not done in the past could be a sign, but it doesn't have to be. In the case of the soldier above, I had read the signs correctly, but he was not prepared to admit the truth until he better understood the person that was asking. Every suicidal ideation is as unique as the individual. What might make one person suicidal wouldn't make you, and vice versa. One person's pain is another person's party. One of my soldiers had suffered from overwhelming thoughts of suicide after his wife left and took their small child. A few months later another soldier's wife left. I asked him if he was thinking of suicide. He responded, "Chaplain, you can come over to my house tonight and bless my party that I am throwing. I have been wanting out of this marriage for three years. Now I can finally get my life back."

Both soldiers that had challenges in their marriages felt safe sharing what they were going through; with one it simply took a little more time to build rapport. Neither felt that they were being judged or would be judged by anything they said. In our workshops and in every intervention, it is my goal to set an environment that clearly says to the person at risk, this is a safe place. Several years ago, in my personal journal I wrote, "I will live by a personal creed that wherever I am, that is the safest place a person can be." Many individuals at risk do not feel they have a safe place to share. For the soldier there is fear that they will lose their job, for the teen there is fear of further alienation. A 19-year-old female was thinking of suicide. She had been in foster care at one time but was now all alone. She was putting herself through her first semester of college and was weary, but still managed to make a 4.0 in her school work. However, it didn't bring her joy because she had no one that celebrated her accomplishments. In her words, "No one hugged me or told me, 'Great job!' or 'I'm proud of you! So, what's the point?" She moved in with an aunt, but the girl's mental health was slipping; with each passing day her resilience waned, and the thoughts of suicide began. The aunt accused her of not being grateful and told her she was a problem. She was not in a safe place.

A 14-year-old boy texted a suicide note to a friend that was passed on to me and the police department. We immediately paid a visit. When the officer mentioned the note, the boy denied that it was his because his mother was present. Seeing that this was not a safe place, I asked if I could visit with the boy one-on-one. In private conversation I asked, "Are you having thoughts of suicide?" He said he was and then shared that his parents didn't understand. They had him taking all advanced classes in school and learning two or three musical instruments. He was glad that he made good grades and could play multiple instruments, but he was also highly stressed. He felt that any sign of weakness was met with disdain by the parents. Additionally, the boy had experienced the loss of a friend to suicide just one month prior. He was not in a safe place.

After our need for air, food, and water according to Abraham Maslow's hierarchy of needs, our greatest and most basic need is safety. In the absence of safety there is little, if any, foundation for the meeting of all other needs. If I am in the middle of a home invasion, I am not really concerned with making it to a community block party on time or whether the beans are cold when I get there. Without safety, every other need or desire is irrelevant. The boy that does not feel emotionally safe to share his feelings with his parents will not see clearly to know that his parents love him deeply. A soldier that has been traumatized by the unsafe conditions of war will continue to experience those feelings in a local restaurant or church setting. The same is true of a woman that has been raped or a child that has been molested.

The power to restore hope is directly proportional to our ability to help others feel safe; doing so can often be a challenge. In every case, such environment is always contingent upon the helper's willingness to step out of their own personal comfort zone into the discomfort zone of others. I would add that restoring hope is not about the words of wisdom you are able to give but the pain you are willing to hear without judgement.

I am reminded of a carpenter who was described as "a man of sorrows and acquainted with grief." He was rejected by those that appeared to be successful, but he was much loved and admired by those that were broken. When he was with broken, hurting people he made them feel safe. They found comfort in his presence and a willingness to share their deepest hurts and longings; he instilled hope.

A willingness to be acquainted with the grief of others is not a burden, but a gift. Having this mindset of a gift rather than a burden is essential to the success of the intervention, but it is so much more. That a person would trust you with their deepest and most difficult thoughts speaks to the nature of your own character. It is a truth that you can draw upon for your own self-care in those times when you are one filled with sorrow over the hurts of so many others, but it is more than that. A willingness to be acquainted with the grief of others is the place where miracles happen. It's the place where those that could not see beyond the moment can begin to see the possibilities of a tomorrow. It's the place where an exchange is made. The person at risk entrusts you with their hopelessness and you help them find hope. They share their pain and you help them find purpose and a passion to live life even with all its challenges. Yes, it is a gift, both the ability to help others and the ability to stand with them as they share their pain.

The color of each section of the model has significance and helps remind us of where we are in our conversation with the person at risk. Listening is yellow for a variety of reasons. Yellow with black letters is one of the easiest color combinations to see from a long distance, it grabs our attention. Yellow road signs remind us to be cautious of ice on bridges and rough roads ahead. Yellow school buses remind us to slow down and take our time so that children are safe. At the same time the model has just enough yellow with a small edge of the model completely trimmed in yellow to indicate that we are always listening. We do not stop listening as we move into learning or leading. The yellow at the very top of the model shows that our listening is more highly focused than it was at the base when we began because we are making sure that the person at risk has accepted the need for safety and that they are willing to take ownership in keeping themselves safe even as others seek to help them too.

An interesting thing about the color yellow is that too much is disturbing. It has been said that babies cry more in rooms that are painted completely yellow. Listening is engaging; we must speak at some point, but it is always measured. We don't want to be like the man whose wife complains that she feels like she is talking to a brick wall. Just enough yellow is refreshing, like a yellow bow in a little girl's hair. As we step into the yellow, we are acknowledging that we need to slow down and be aware of our surroundings and of what is going on in the life of the person at risk. We need to listen, but we must also engage with words that build rapport and strengthen the feeling of safety for the one we are helping. We will consider the significance of the colors brown and green in the model in the chapters that follow.

Good listeners build rapport, and rapport can be developed far more quickly than most people assume. For a good exercise in personal self-awareness, you might ask a friend or perhaps an acquaintance in the office, "Do I present myself as an approachable person?" If they hesitate to respond, you might consider ways that you can improve your rapport building skill, as it is an essential key to a successful intervention. Part of building rapport includes an awareness of cultural differences that play a part in communication with others. For example, the Asian culture as compared to the American culture is more reserved. Getting to the truth of life and death issues may take more time with a person at risk that is Asian, because while truth is important, there is a high regard for proper respect. Being direct can be perceived as rude or offensive. Asking, "Are you thinking of suicide?" is a very direct question which might be perceived as confrontational in an Asian culture. While the *Listen Learn Lead* model discourages confrontation, this is especially so in helping individuals of different cultures.

So how do we move forward? Again, slowly, and appropriately. I will share this thought often, but it certainly applies here. Often, I preface the question with the statement, "Sometimes when a person is facing challenges like what you are facing, they may have thoughts of suicide." Pause… "Are you having thoughts of suicide?" The statement destigmatizes the question in advance by letting the person know that others have had similar thoughts and it is not unusual to have such thoughts if they are.

There is another aspect of culture that we need to consider that can sometimes be missed when we are considering risk. We will call our fictitious suicide victim Lou. Lou is a great person, highly respected in his community, his kids are in private school, he has a lovely wife, a beautiful home, plenty of money and no mental or physical health challenges. He is the least likely person in the world to take his own life (in our minds). However, Lou's boss is a patronizing narcissist. Company morale is horrible, there is no financial transparency and rather than promoting competent employees from within, the boss hires family members that do his bidding without question, often to the detriment of fellow employees and the good of the company. Unfortunately, Lou works in an extremely toxic environment.

In 2010 then-Brigadier General Peter Bayer wanted to know why so many soldiers were killing themselves in Iraq or shortly after returning home. He asked Dave Matsuda, PhD for help. After extensive interviews with unit members, battle buddies, and family, Matsuda concluded that a significant number of suicides were triggered by toxic command climate. Toxic work environments can cause physical and mental health challenges.

I worked my way through college as a summer and holiday employee of Eastern Airlines. After it was liquidated in 1991 under Chapter 11 bankruptcy, several employees within the Atlanta hub took their lives within the year. What had been the third largest airline in the world and a wonderful place to work for a college kid, spiraled to nothing, taking lives with it. Toxic work environments are deadly even when all else in a person's life appears to be healthy.

In 2010 Bernie Madoff was sentenced to 150 years in prison for his billion-dollar Ponzi scheme. He financially ruined countless individuals and families with fraudulent investments. At least four suicides are directly related to the harm that he caused, including his own son. Over the past decade, at least 21 reality tv stars have died by suicide. Admittedly, these shows often thrive on the toxic environment they can create for TV ratings. Toxic cultures can take place in the military, law enforcement, corporations, schools, churches, little league teams and families.

After working one-on-one for several weeks with a veteran, his wife finally joined us at the table. As she attempted to share her side of the story, he yelled out in a fit of rage, "You are a F---ing liar!" He was so loud that the receptionist down the hall almost called the police, as she was concerned for everyone's safety. It was in that moment that I completely understood why the wife had a restraining order against her husband. He never did own up to how he was creating a toxic home environment. It felt like a scene from the 1994 movie, Gaslight. Gaslighting is a common technique used by abusers in a marriage relationship to gain power or maintain control.

As we seek to help the person at risk we should be aware of the toxic environment they have been exposed to and provide them with a safe environment in which to express the struggles or challenges that have brought them to the point of suicide. As we seek to build rapport we should also consider the volume and the speed of our words. Taking our que from an ancient Proverb, "A gentle answer turns away wrath", we don't want to be loud and we certainly don't want to mock, "Oh my God, I can't believe you are thinking of suicide. Why in the world would you have thoughts like that?" In considering the speed of your words, your best choice is to mirror their speed; too fast sounds like a sales pitch and too slow is condescending.

I was pleasantly surprised recently to discover the existence of the International Listening Association (ILA). The organization was founded in 1979 by Dr. Ralph G. Nichols, who was a professor at the University of Minnesota. The organization has grown into an international community working in more than 19 countries promoting the study of listening. The ILA points out two helpful listening behaviors when interacting with the bereaved. First, provide the opportunity to ventilate, and second, provide presence, ("being there").[i] A person that is suicidal may be bereaved about many things, not just the loss of a loved one. It may be the loss of a marriage, a job, a child etc. The ILA also suggests that in spoken message 55% of the meaning is translated non-verbally, 38% is indicated by the tone of voice, while only 7% is conveyed by the words used.[ii]

I never had a course on listening, counseling yes, but listening, well let's just say that has taken a lifetime to learn. In college we take courses on marketing and communication, it's all about what we have to say and how we are going to say it. Then we graduate and join the local Toast Masters to further our talking skills. In the work of suicide intervention, the greater skill is the ability to listen and, when it is necessary to speak, to do so in a compassionate tone that conveys safety and support. I keep a letter from a veteran's wife in my top desk drawer that reads simply, "Thank you for being there at midnight when I didn't know what to do. My husband is alive today because you cared." Seminary students know this as the ministry of presence.

Active listening is not easy work. If it were simply a matter of reflecting back what you have heard, we could solve many problems and close every counseling center by replacing people with parrots. Listening in a manner that helps the person at risk of suicide means putting away our own bias and checking our emotional responses, not that every emotional response is bad, but we want to be certain that any emotional response we give is moving us in the right direction. Empathy would be a good emotional response. We must also be in tune with both verbal and nonverbal communication and it is more than just parroting what has already been said.

When do we ask, "the question"?

The question of suicide moves the conversation to the pivotal point, a crossroad between a bad decision and a better decision. We must come to the crossroad or there is no intervention. But when do we ask the question? My short answer is sooner than later. When you are aware of risk and/or you see signs, begin a caring conversation, take a few minutes to build rapport and ask – are you having thoughts of suicide? Remember, risks are the circumstances of life in which a person finds themselves. It does not mean that the person is thinking of suicide. It simply means that the potential is present. Signs are the things that people at risk might do that they typically don't do or anything out of character with their normal way of being.

- Giving away things
- Sleeping too little or too much
- Negative self-talk
- Increase in alcohol
- Strange social media posts
- Outbursts of anger
- Withdrawing from others
- Any mood changes

The above are just a few examples of signs; there are others. I was in one of the gyms in my hometown speaking with personal trainers about coming to a workshop. I told them that they could even receive CE credit for the Trainer certification. One of the trainers commented, "Why would I come to a suicide intervention workshop? My clients aren't suicidal; they are all trying to get healthy." Is that so? I know a veteran that ran the treadmill up as high as he could to induce what he hoped would be a fatal heart attack. Thankfully, he was not successful. A friend that trains elite bodybuilders called me concerned about one of his clients. She was suicidal because she had been informed by her doctor that she had cancer. She spiraled into depression saying she would rather die than have her body destroyed by chemo and cancer. Everyone in the gym is not healthy. I shared a few more thoughts, and one of the trainers said, "You know, come to think of it, I do feel like a therapist with many of my clients." Yes, and so does the barber and the bartender, two professions that thrive on the ability to build rapport.

I called my oldest son, MaCrae, who had recently arrived at Charleston Air Force Base to let him know that we would be coming down from Ft. Jackson with the Chaplain team to conduct Dignified Transfer exercises. I had not seen MaCrae since Chad had been injured six months earlier. He had no idea of the overwhelming darkness that invaded my mind. After the exercise our team had the opportunity to eat lunch with a World War II Medal of Honor recipient. I asked MaCrae to join us. He was so excited being able to eat lunch with a war hero, military brass and yes, his dad. After lunch we toured the USS Yorktown. As we walked the decks of the old ship the following conversation took place.

Son: Dad, when was the last time you were in the gym?

Me: Uh…it's been a while…

Son: How's Chad doing?

Me: He's much better. He was fortunate. We saw some kids in Cincinnati that weren't so lucky.

Son: Well Dad, I know that Chad's accident was tough. You were the one there when it happened...

Me: Yeah, it bothers me. He got hurt on my watch and I couldn't stop it.

Son: Mom told me the Shriners took care of all the expenses in Cincinnati. What about the hospital in Atlanta?

Me: They were ruthless in wanting their money. I tried to work with them, but they were not interested in helping me, even though they helped a room full of people with benevolence the day I went to talk with them. They showed no mercy on helping with our bills.

Son: Dad, I know you have been through a lot the past few years and then with Chad getting hurt, that was tough.

Me: Yes, it was...

Son: I also know that you have always loved being in the gym and you are the one who gave me the love that I have for working out, but you are not working out anymore?

Me: It's not that I don't want to; I haven't had it in me to do it. It just seems like it doesn't matter anymore.

[At this point MaCrae stops walking and ask me to step over to the side away from the foot traffic]

Son: Based on everything you have told me I am wondering if you are having thoughts of suicide?

Me: Yes MaCrae, I have.

Son: Dad, first I want you to know that I love you very much and I know you feel like you have been kicked in the gut. You have had a lot of difficult things happen in your life even before Chad got hurt. But none of those things are a reason to take your life. We can get through this, I am here for you. I don't want you to take your life.

We talked several more minutes and as we did I could sense a window of resilience cracking open. Hope was beginning to stir once again in my heart. I got back on the bus with my team for the 150-mile drive back to Ft. Jackson. The next day at 0600, I was putting my PT gear on for the morning PT formation and run. There was a knock at my door. I opened the door and MaCrae was standing there in his Air Force PT uniform. He had gotten permission from his Flight Leader to make the drive to Jackson to check on his dad. He, an E-3 Airman, did PT that morning with a company of Army Chaplains. He never left my side, staying with me through the entire duty day. When the workday was done he said, "Dad, get your sweats on; we are going to the gym." MaCrae was a 19-year-old Airman with perhaps two hours of mandatory training in suicide intervention compliments of the US Air Force. It was enough to save his dad's life.

Even though I didn't realize that I was putting off any signs, what MaCrae noticed was the fact that I was not going to the gym anymore. He knew that for more than 30 years I had been an avid gym enthusiast, bringing him into the fold at the age of 13. I had even trained Chad in setting state and national powerlifting records. No longer doing what you have loved doing most of your life is a subtle sign that can often be overlooked. Thankfully, MaCrae didn't miss it; he was also aware of the circumstances. Chad's injury was the culmination of several events that had occurred in my life over a period of 15 years that had carved a hole in my foundation of resilience and left me with many questions. What I have learned since then is that while life can be filled with questions, some questions are filled with life. Ironically, asking the suicide question is one of them.

Often, as in the case with my son, the helper may already know much of the backstory. The *Listen Learn Lead* model is fluid in this regard, rather than linear. But the moment the question is asked, we move into learning within the model. As we will see in the next chapter, in the learning phase there is still much to be discovered in working with the person at risk. It is not only what we learn, but perhaps most importantly what the hurting person begins to learn.

Listen Summary

- Listening answers the *WHAT* question
- There may not be signs; be aware of circumstances
- Create a safe environment through a caring conversation
- Preface the suicide question with the statement: Sometimes when people have challenges and difficulties like you are experiencing, they have thoughts of suicide. Are you have having thoughts of suicide?

LEARN

Hello darkness, my old friend,
I've come to talk with you again.
Paul Simon, Music Artist

I have asked the suicide question thousands of times, and in almost every instance, the person's head comes up, and they look me in the eye, often for the first time. It is as if I have reached down in the core of their being and touched their soul. It may be the first hello they have had in sometime from the light instead of the darkness, where they have spent time often. Asking a person if they are thinking of suicide is a simple question, one that opens the door to hope, one that saves lives; yet few ever ask the question, though the other desperately wishes they would.

Many people mistakenly believe that asking the question will put the thought in a person's mind. I will address this question in further detail later. For now, imagine that you are walking with a friend in the park. You see two people on bikes headed in your direction. Your friend begins to step off the path into the wood line when you notice a coiled-up rattlesnake just four feet behind her in the leaves. "Mary don't take another step backwards. Come toward me carefully and as quickly as possible." You were aware of the danger before Mary was and your knowledge of the circumstances helped to raise Mary's awareness of the danger which kept her from the harm she may have experienced. I am convinced that before suicide is a conscious thought, it is wreaking havoc in our subconscious through the negative self-talk we give ourselves, the difficult circumstances we find ourselves in and the challenges that strain our coping capabilities.

We move into the learning phase of the *Listen Learn Lead* model by asking the question, "Are you having thoughts of suicide?" If the Listening phases properly addresses the *What* question by making us aware that something is going on, the learning phase will address the *why*. That doesn't necessarily mean that we use the word, *why* with the person at risk, but it is the point were the helper begins to gain further insight into the circumstances that have brought about the thoughts of suicide as they hear the story behind the pain.

Some mistakingly believe that we should avoid the use of *why* questions because it may invalidate the person at risk and place the person asking in a position that they really shouldn't be in, as if the helper has all the answers. Why questions are appropriate in the right context, but in a crisis moment between life and death, it may not be helpful.

As a person of faith, I recognize one of the titles of Jesus as the *Wonderful Counselor,* the master at asking great questions, and yes, he did use *why* questions quite often. However, you would notice in the Bible that in the three dozen times he did use *why* it was most often in a confrontive way. There is a place in counseling for confrontation, but *Listen Learn Lead* is not counseling, it is first aid, so we want to avoid confrontation to the best of our ability. When our oldest son was five, he fell from the top of his swingset and and broke his leg. The important question for mom at the moment was not, "Why did you do this?" but rather, "What do we need to do now?" The immediate moment of crisis was not the time for confronation; that came six weeks later after the cast was off, and he wanted to return to the top of his swingset. Think of the learning phase as an expansion of the listening phase that addresses what's going on. In the learning phase you learn their why.

Don't over think your words; it will cause paralysis by analysis. Be natural, and show that you care by maintaining a calm disposition. There have been many times when I have slipped up and asked a why question; it's OK. You may have also heard that all your questions should be open-ended questions. The argument is that closed ended questions do not open up conversation. But there is a place for closed ended questions just as there is for *why* questions. You see a co-worker crying in the break room after a cursing repremand from the supervisor. Sure, you could say,

"Geewiz, why was the boss acting like that?" However, a better question might be "Sue, are you OK?" It's a closed ended question, but it does establish that you are concerned. You might then follow up with, "I can see that was a painful experience, and I just want you to know I care. I'm here for you if you want to talk."

Much of the helper's learning takes place in the listening phase. The one that is truly learning the most in the Learn phase is the person at risk. Perhaps the best way to understand this concept is by examining an actual intervention verbatim. I was sitting on a Southwest flight preparing to head to Arkansas, via Dallas. I was rather excited sitting in a half full plane on an empty row all to myself; finally, plenty of room and an opportunity to catch a nap. As the doors began to close, the last passenger rushed in. As he walked past several empty aisles I thought, "Surely, he will sit down somewhere before he gets to my row," but no. The man came right to my aisle. I looked up almost in shock as he asked, "May I join you?" I didn't say what I was thinking. I said, "Sure" and moved over one seat to the window. I had a flashback to the monologue in the movie *The Christmas Story* after the dogs had torn through the house and stolen the Christmas turkey. "It was gone, all gone! No turkey! No turkey sandwiches! No turkey salad! No turkey gravy! Turkey Hash! Turkey A La King! Or gallons of turkey soup! Gone, ALL GONE!" Well at least I might still get the nap, but that wasn't to be either. Here's how the conversation went after the man who appeared to be about my age sat down.

Passenger: Headed home?

Me: No, I am headed to teach a workshop in Arkansas. How about you?

Passenger: I live in Dallas...So, you're a teacher; what do you teach?

[At this point I know I have a 50/50 chance that I might be able to get out of the conversation so that I can start my nap. Whenever I mention suicide half the people quickly conclude the conversation and with the other half, it is like opening Pandora's box, and they want to talk about all the miseries and evils of the world.]

Me: Uh...I teach classes...

Passenger: What kind of classes?

Me: [Rolling the dice in my head] uh...Suicide intervention...

[Ah yes, the bet paid off. Total silence followed...but only for about a minute]

Passenger: I guess it was meant for me to sit with you today.

Thus, began a 90-minute conversation that ended in the Dallas Airport with a call to one of his friends that assured me he would be waiting at the man's house when he got home to further help him stay safe. In this instance, it was the person at risk that instigated movement into the suicide intervention model; this is often the case. It was for me that day, as all I was thinking about was a nap. The conversation continued...

Me: So, what's going on?

Within ten minutes I had discovered that the man was fifty years old. He had been dating a lady for several years, but she finally called it off and took a job in Atlanta. Three weeks after his mother passed, the man had flown to Atlanta to ask for the lady's hand in marriage. She turned him down saying, "I have a life now without you and I refuse to be your mother substitute."

Me: I can imagine that all of this has been painful for you. So, help me understand, with everything that has happened are you having thoughts of suicide? [in this case I already knew the answer based on his comments.]

Passenger: Yes, I have; I think that is why I am supposed to be sitting next to you.

Me: It sounds like there is a part of you that wants to live?

Passenger: I guess so, but my mom is gone, and my woman is gone....

Me: Do you have a plan?

Passenger: A plan?

Me: Do you have a plan to end your life?

Passenger: I did this morning, but now I'm not so sure.

Me: What was that plan?

Passenger: I'm from Texas. I have guns….

From this conversation you can see that getting to the suicide question happened rather quickly. In fact, the wheels of the plane were just coming off the ground in Atlanta as I was asking the suicide question. We spent the remainder of the flight to Dallas discussing ways that he might rediscover hope, life, and a future. I also asked him if he was a person of faith. Finding that he was opened dialogue into further resources he could utilize in rebuilding his personal resilience. The final resource that I left him as I waited for my next flight was to connect him with his own friend that I spoke with on his phone. The man gave me permission to share the conversation that we had just been in, and the friend promised to meet the man at his house, secure his weapons and follow through with making sure that he contacted a counselor in their community.

What did the man at risk learn? First, he was becoming aware of a renewed sense of purpose in his life. Twice he said, "There was a *reason* I felt led to sit next to you," when there were dozens of other seats available; those are statements filled with purpose. Second, he was beginning to understand that someone cared. I did care, even though I had hoped to take a nap. The instant he broke the momentary silence, I was in the model. I was in the right place at the right time, the nap could wait.

As you look at the diagram of the model you will notice that it is made up of three concentric triangles with the yellow listen section going all the way to the top. This is indicative of the fact that as caregivers we are always listening. We never stop listening as we move through the model. Yes, the helper is learning, yes, we are leading, but both are embedded in listening. In counseling hundreds of soldiers, one of the universal themes that seems to come through is this idea that no one is listening to me. Many times, the person at risk might feel like the one in Paul Simon's *Sound of Silence*; they are surrounded by people that *hear without listening* and their only *friend is darkness.*

Shortly after the death of a 14-year-old in my hometown I received a copy of what appeared to be a final text from another teen in our community. It read in part, "I know that some people are questioning my decision, and I don't want people to wonder why I did this. I honestly don't know how and when it started. All I knew was that it was there. Over time this darkness followed and grew, wanting more attention. One of my friends noticed this and started to talk to me. I denied it, the fact I have this darkness following me, but he knew, so I decided to talk to him. It really helped, and sometimes the conversation got really deep and dark. He was even more help than the therapist because he gets me. He gets me because he was going through it like I was except I didn't know, no one knew, and several weeks later he committed suicide…He didn't leave any reasoning so it's still a possibility that it's my fault…The darkness is now a part of me, and it will always be with me. This darkness is also causing a feeling of evil inside me. Very malicious feelings that want to hurt things, and I don't want to hurt anything.

To make sure I don't hurt anything the only thing/least I can do is killing myself…I hope this letter provides the justification of why I'm doing this. If it doesn't, I hope that you guys can at least forgive me."

The young man that texted the message was overwhelmed with feelings of guilt and shame and was blaming himself for his friend's death. In many ways this teen is like hundreds of veterans that I have worked with that blame themselves for the death of a team member. Thankfully, the teen that received the text shared it with his mother, who shared it with one of my associates that then sent it to me. As quickly as possible I made my way to the home. As of the writing of this book, the teen is still alive. His parents understand the situation, and he is getting the help he needs.

The learning section of the model is Brown; indicating feelings of wholeness and connection; there is greater approachability with those that wear brown. It is a warm color that helps with relaxation which increases learning. Asking the suicide question moves us into the brown, that place where, for the first time in a while the person at risk may feel connected to someone else.

As I was penning this section of the book, my phone rang. For the next 45 minutes I was in a conversation with a man that said, "I have always been on my own, I have always been able to do things without help." But now this man is feeling like a failure; he is having thoughts of suicide. I shared with him that he didn't have to go through this alone. People love him; his family loves him. We are here for him. He felt broken, but he doesn't have to carry the broken pieces by himself. As we talked he felt the warmth of the conversation. He was sensing a connection because I was willing to ask the suicide question.

In the morning session of a workshop, a distinguished gentleman sat on the front row. He was highly engaged throughout the first half. During a break I discovered that he was a Colonel with multiple deployments. After lunch I was chatting with a few others in the parking lot. I saw him park his car, but his gait was slow and lethargic as he walked with a downcast head. When he passed by, I said, "Sir, how was lunch?" He responded, "Chaplain, you got a minute?" I disengaged from the group and instructed my co-facilitator to start the afternoon session. We moved under a large Elm to get out of the sun. "What's up, Sir?" He quickly responded, "My wife just served me with divorce papers." The following conversation ensued.

Me: I'm sorry to hear that, Sir? That must have made for a difficult lunchtime. Is this something you were expecting?

Col: I guess I was hoping it wouldn't come to this, but Chaplain, I have to say I'm not surprised.

Me: What led up to this announcement today?

The Colonel went on to explain that he had been involved in multiple deployments and losses. He had been in therapy, anger management, seen his priest, and tried to do everything he was asked to do.

Me: Well, Sir, you know what I do for a living. Based on everything you have told me I need to ask you a question. Are you having thoughts of suicide?

Col: I have been for the past three years.

Me: So, compared to times past, how do you feel today?

Col: It's about the worst it has ever been.

Me: So, if you don't have your relationship with your wife you would be willing to take your life?

[I could see that he was pondering the question. I asked another question.]

Me: What other relationships do you have in your life?

Col: I have five boys.

Me: Wow that's great. I have four boys of my own. Tell me about your sons.

For the next few minutes he shared with me about his awesome sons. One was an Eagle Scout, one a member of a champion lacrosse team, another, an expert fly fisherman, the two youngest were strong academically and in the gym. As he shared, I could literally see his countenance transforming. He had been slouching, but now his shoulders were back, and his chin was up. He was looking me in the eye and there seemed to be a twinkle of pride in his own as he told me about his boys.

Me: This afternoon I'll be getting on a plane to fly 1,200 miles back home. There is not much I can do if anything to help restore your marriage, but marriage or no marriage, it sounds like you have some incredible reasons to stay alive.

The Colonel was agreeing with me before I finished the sentence - he had at least five. The encounter with the Colonel occurred four years ago, he is still alive.

From a mountain that compensates for the curvature of the horizon, scientists tell us that a sharp eye could see a single candle on a dark night more than 30 miles away. The *Listen Learn Lead* model is shaped as a triangle to remind us that we must climb the mountain to see the one solitary candle in the distance. Asking the suicide question moves us half way up the mountain and the person at risk begins to see light.

The South Base Camp for Mt. Everest is in Nepal, and the North Base Camp is in Tibet. Both camps are at an altitude of more than 17,000 feet, a little more than half way up the mountain to the peak at 29,000 feet. Getting to the Learn phase of the model, like getting up to the Base Camp at Everest is hard work in and of itself. Many people that could otherwise help often never get to this phase because they refuse to ask the question that gets them there. But those that do find resources to help them make it the rest of the way. Most often it is the person at risk that provides the resources or motivation the helper needs as they are invited to share their story. Sometimes those resources are strong (five boys that fill a father's heart with pride) and other times we must listen longer to find resources (the homeless vet who has no family and few friends).

Over the years I have spent time with hundreds of homeless vets. Many have incredible stories. They were heroic individuals; their resilience amazes me. Despite overwhelming challenges, they are making it with what they have. Others have not been so fortunate, often they would sit in silence, not wanting to talk. When they did talk it was about not being able to find help or how the VA had turned them down. Broken systems cannot heal broken people, only people can do that. There was a time when I expended much energy trying to fix whatever system I was dealing with. I have in recent years realized that the best thing I can do is work with people rather than systems, and perhaps within that, teaching others how to listen is my greatest work. Often when we listen there is silence; don't be afraid of it. You can learn a lot in the silence and so can the person at risk.

After a horrible automobile accident that left his sister fatally injured, the brother who had been a co-passenger expressed thoughts of suicide to his mother. He felt responsible for letting them both get in the car with a drunk driver. The mother asked me to come to the house, and she left so that I could speak with her son in confidence. I sat in the living room while the young man sat in his room knowing I was there. After 30 minutes he came out and sat on the couch. He didn't say a word, nor did I. Another 15 minutes went by, and he finally spoke, "Why are you here?" I simply responded, "Because I don't want you to die." More silence, and then he began to cry. In many ways the conversation that followed was like ones I have already shared. The lesson here, silence can often be golden. The silence demonstrated to the person at risk that I was with him, even without words. Again, the ministry of presence is a key; it is "being" rather than "doing."

As we have made clear, asking the suicide question is the means for moving into the learning phase. So why then do many people struggle to ask this very important question? For some, it may be that they just don't realize they need to ask. Even with the man on the plane I asked the question, though we both knew that suicide was the subject at hand. Asking the question grants permission. It lets the person know that you know. It demonstrates care, that you are the one they are safe to express their deepest hurts with, and it confirms that we are indeed talking about suicide. We will consider further reasons for hesitation in the Questions chapter. For now, understand that asking the suicide question is the springboard for moving into learning.

In the learning phase we gain greater insight into their why. It is also the place where, perhaps for the first time, the person at risk begins to understand that someone is willing to listen, willing to learn why they feel as they do. As we listen, we learn of possible motivations in the person's life that can encourage them to choose life. By asking the Colonel what other relationships he had I discovered his five incredible boys. Asking about his boys filled him with positive memories and pride over their accomplishments. But there have been other instances that were not so easy. Working with a homeless Marine without any family was a tremendous challenge. Granted, I don't like to play the guilt card, but when he said, "No one would care if I died." The only thing I could say in that moment was, "I would." I paused for a moment and continued, "Let's find a way to get past where you are. There are other Marines that need you."

In the learning phase the person at risk comes face to face with the reality that their life is at risk. They begin to understand that suicide is not the solution to their problem. I was speaking one night to a group of 70 high school students. After I finished my 20-minute message, a 14-year-old girl wanted to talk. Immediately she said, "I realize tonight my life is at risk." I asked her if she was having thoughts of suicide, and she said yes. She then shared with me all the reasons that she was feeling as she did. The last word she shared was, "I feel like such a coward for feeling this way." I responded by saying, "Sweetheart, you are the most courageous young lady I have ever met. You just shared your story with someone you don't even know. That takes great courage." This young lady learned that night that she was more courageous than she realized. It takes courage to ask for help. She also realized how dangerously close she was to the rattlesnake of suicide. The incident with this young lady happened four years ago. In 2017 she invited Sherry and me to her high school graduation.

Some may argue that there is no real risk of suicide if a person could say, "I realize tonight my life is at risk." These are likely the same people that are surprised when they receive news that someone has died by suicide. From all the experiences that I have had, and the lessons learned, I am honestly not surprised when I hear of another suicide, especially when I can do a bit of forensics into the circumstances leading up to the event. Suicide is a normal thought in abnormal situations. When coping abilities are taxed beyond limits I naturally assume that there is the possibility of the presence of suicidal thoughts. In fact, I am surprised when such is not the case. When a person comes to a conscious awareness of their risk it does not increase the risk, but it has the opposite effect. Awareness decreases risk. Just because a person doesn't realize that they are at risk doesn't mean that they aren't. A person walking and talking on his phone unaware of an open manhole cover ten yards ahead does not decrease his risk by being unaware of the fact. One of my boys is a much safer driver after coming close to death in an accident that totaled his truck. His awareness level has greatly increased, and he drives much more defensively today. When the person at risk of suicide can articulate that they realize their life is at risk, then they are able to take steps that build in safety through community resources that strengthen resilience and defend against potential dangers.

One final and important thought for this chapter bears repeating. In learning their *why*, it is imperative that we listen without judgment. I shared with a class of law enforcement officers about two veterans that were suicidal. The first, after his Martin guitar was stolen, and the second after the county animal control took her dog from her. A participant made the comment, "You're joking right. Why would that cause anyone to be suicidal?" (I couldn't help but think of Paul Harvey and his radio show.) Before the story had been told the participant had already formed a judgement. He didn't know the story. He had not walked in the shoes of those that had experienced loss. To him the loss of a guitar or a pet was not anything that would cause him to be suicidal so why should it cause someone else? Then I shared the histories of these two veterans. The first was a Marine that was serving in Beirut when the barracks were bombed on October 23, 1983. More than 300 people died that day including 241 Marines. At the time the guitar was stolen the Marine was living in a homeless shelter. The guitar was all he had left that brought meaning to his life. The second veteran was also homeless, living in the woods near a park. A citizen called the pound complaining about the dog. Rather than help the veteran find shelter, the only thing which brought meaning to her life was taken from here. As Harvey would say, "And now you know the rest of the story." When we are quick to judge others because of the things that have destroyed their resilience and will to live, it is difficult if not impossible to build rapport that has the potential to restore hope and rebuild resilience.

In the next chapter the learning will continue as we move into the leading phase and the final step in the *Listen Learn Lead* model.

Learn Summary

- We are learning their why
- They are learning that someone cares
- We are finding stepping stones that will move us into leading
- We must maintain a nonjudgmental attitude

LEAD

*The purpose of human life is to serve, and to
show compassion and the will to help others.*
Albert Schweitzer

Leading others to safety when their hope and
resilience have failed them is compassion in its
highest form. So, the green color within the
model for the leading phase would probably seem
somewhat obvious. It happens every Spring, plants
green up, and the grass begins to grow. Green is
associated with life, growth, hope and a future. Leading
is embedded in Listening and Learning, which we never
stop doing as we move through the model. We simply
become more focused in our listening and learning as
we move into leading. The Leading phase addresses the
How questions. How do you plan to end your life, and
how can we keep you safe for now?

In the learning phase we have gained insight into the
reasons the person is having suicidal thoughts. We have

also discovered potential stepping stones for considering reasons to live. We move into the leading phase by asking, "Do you have a plan to end your life?" Our goal is to lead them away from self-harm by disengaging the means of ending life. The model is incomplete if we fail to discover the means.

Some may argue that individuals that show signs or make any direct cries for help are not serious about suicide. This is an assumption that we should avoid. A dear friend continues to deal with his anger that the system let him down. Randy had tried on many occasions to get his son, Tyler help. He felt that those who could have helped did not show proper care or take his son's cries seriously. Over a period of several years Tyler had shown signs and even made attempts. On his eighth attempt he died. Every cry for help should be taken seriously.

A man caught in a riptide with his arms flailing as he thrashes in the current pulling him toward danger is a sign that someone needs to help. We don't need to wait and see if he is able to articulate that he is drowning; the risk is already there. The same is true of a person having a heart attack or individuals involved in automobile accidents.

Sherry and I came upon a car carrying four teenage boys that had just missed the curve, rolled down the bank near a bridge and into a creek. One boy was badly injured, two were pouring beer into the creek to conceal the evidence, and one appeared dazed and confused. When I tried to help him up the bank he had no grip.

He started to faint. When I finally eased him down on the curb I noticed that his pupils were dilated, and his breathing and pulse were rapid. When I asked him his name, he couldn't talk. He did reach in his pocket and give me his wallet, which at the time I thought was odd. Interestingly, he was the only one that did not reek of alcohol. The teen was suffering from shock, which left untreated can be deadly. He was not able to articulate his name or what happened, but it was obvious to me that he was in an accident. In a similar way, those at risk of suicide are often not able to articulate that they are suicidal. However, they may say or do things that are odd or out of character. The most important part of leading as caregivers is the ability to recognize signs that others fail to see. Intervention is more than being ready and willing; we must also be able. Otherwise we are like the thousands that pass by the scene of an accident, and all we can do is stream it live on our social media to let others know we were there. When it comes to suicide intervention there is more to it than simply being present – We must lead. There is something we must do.

One night I received a call from a man in another state. We had the following conversation.

Helper: Hello.

Caller: What's your name?

Helper: My name is Ken. What's your name?

Caller: It's Ronald McDonald; how's that?

Helper: All right, Ronald. How can I help you?

Caller: I don't know…just hoping I guess…. [Ambivalence]

Helper: What is it that you are hoping, Ronald?

Caller: Well, I guess I was hoping that there is a reason for everything….

Helper: Help me understand what you mean by that.

Caller: It just seems like nothing makes sense anymore…. the VA screwed me on my disability. I can't think straight. I need surgery on my back…. I don't think you or anyone else can help. NO BODY CARES!

Helper: I'm sorry that you are having trouble. Are you in physical pain right now?

Caller: Yes Sir, whenever I forget my meds and now I am out…and the engine blew on my car, and I can't even go and get more.

Helper: So, you don't have your meds, your car is broken down, and you need surgery, but the VA has let you down.

Caller: You could say that!

Helper: Thank you for helping me to get a better picture of your situation. Now help me understand…are you really Ronald McDonald?

Caller: Might as well be because life is a cruel joke….

Helper: So, what is your real name?

Caller: I'm Sergeant First Class Troy Jett [not his real name], 75th Ranger Regiment.... Or at least that's who I use to be...But I am nothing and nobody now...A fitting end to a bad life....

Helper: Troy, it sounds like you are talking about suicide. Are you having thoughts of suicide?

Caller: It's more than a thought. I have my 380 right here in front of me. And I bet you're going to say, "DON'T DO IT. You have too much to live for. You'll end up in hell."

Helper: Troy, the truth is I don't want you to end your life...

Caller: But why would you care...Nobody Cares.... It doesn't matter.

Helper: Troy, I can tell you are in a lot of pain right now. The pain is hitting you physically, mentally, emotionally, and maybe even spiritually. But I am also sensing that there is a part of you that wants to live.

Caller: How can you tell that?

Helper: Well, you did call me, right?

Caller: Yes Sir?

Helper: So, the fact that you called tells me that there is a part of you that wants to live. But right now, all the pain that you are experiencing is keeping you from thinking straight. That's what I heard you say. You also said that nothing makes sense anymore. Right?

Caller: Yes Sir, that's right.

Helper: So, making a huge decision about living or dying shouldn't be done when we aren't able to think straight. Would you agree?

Caller: But it's never going to get better.

Helper: Troy, if you end your life, you will never know if things could get better. Would you agree?

Caller: I guess…

Helper: So where are you right now?

Caller: My apartment.

Helper: Where is that?

Caller: 123 A Street.

Helper: What city is that?

[Caller tells me a city 150 miles away. From my wife's phone I immediately make a call directly to the Police Department in his city. I intermittently mute the caller to let the officer know what is happening, and they listen.]

Helper: Is anyone else there with you?

Caller: No, just me.

Helper: Ok, so let's make sure that we get you to a safe place tonight. You live at 123 A Street in Birmingham; is that right?

Caller: What... are you calling the cops?

Helper: Troy, my concern is keeping you safe right now. Then we can look for better ways to relieve the pain.

Caller: So, what are you saying?

Helper: Will you do something for me? Leave your weapon on the table and step away from it. Turn all your lights on in the house, open your front door and have a seat somewhere in your living room away from your weapon. Can you do that for me?

Caller: OK

Helper: Now I have some people on the other line. They are sending help to your apartment right now. I am going to stay on the line with you until they get there. When they arrive, let them in. OK?

Caller: OK

Helper: Troy, I am glad you called me tonight. This is a big step for you and I want to encourage you that it is the right step.

Caller: I hope so...

In this incident, that officer on the other line did an excellent job of listening, at one point providing encouragement to the caller that they would help him.

For the next 15 minutes until EMS arrived, I and the officer remained on the phone. The caller did as I asked him to do, and he is still alive today. You will notice that I also deflected away from any potential argument about who cared or why I needed to call the police. We do not want to argue with those that are at risk, we want to support them.

Lynn Bradley shared with me a call that he took two weeks after attending a workshop. Lynn and his wife run an SOS (Survivors of Suicide) Support group in his church. The caller spoke covertly that she was seeking help for her children. Initially Lynn thought that perhaps her husband had died, and the children needed support in their grief. As he continued to listen, it became evident that the husband had not died by suicide but had abandoned the family, leaving them with little or no financial support. He also discovered that the caller had attempted suicide just three days earlier and was planning again. In her suicide note to the children she was going to encourage them to contact Lynn who would know how to help them. Lynn did a three-way call with the Georgia Crisis Line and was able to get a Response Team to her house as he stayed on the line listening to the Crisis Line worker provide further assistance to the caller. In this case the call was not a cry for help, but a preparation for suicide. Lynn was able to transform the call into an intervention because he was listening and alert to what was really happening. He told me later that the training he had received just two weeks earlier had helped raise his awareness to what was really happening, and that is what helped him help the person in need. Lynn did an excellent job leading this caller to safety and courageously saved a life.

While it may be true that 1 in 20 people have thoughts of suicide every year, thankfully for most, it has only been a passing thought with no plan attached. When this is the case, we can then move quickly into the second how question, "So, how can we keep you safe moving forward?" You may have ideas of how that question should be answered. Don't be overly eager to give pat answers; it will come across as insincere. Instead, pause and let them answer. In this way, it is their decision, a safety plan with buy in because it is what they know they need to do. You are simply providing support to what they know and are willing to do, thus the reason for the "we" in the question.

Who else have you told about your thoughts? This is another helpful question to ask during the leading phase. This question gives us a gage to the possibility of other resources. Many times, the person at risk may say no one else. The follow up question might then be, "Who can we tell that can help?" These questions not only provide the person at risk with resources but the helper as well.

If, as some researchers believe, 50% of suicides happen within minutes of having the thought, then it is also true that 50% have given much thought, perhaps even months considering how they will end their lives. They may have a well thought out plan. The soldier that intended to run himself into a fatal heart attack on the gym's treadmill was concerned that his family would not receive the life insurance proceeds if it was proven to be suicide. He was planning on a more passive means. He also hoped that there would be a liability claim against the gym that would further help his family. Thankfully, his attempt failed, and he was able to receive the help he needed to move beyond thoughts of suicide.

Again, if the research is true, we can deduce that at least 50% of the time an alert helper can intervene long before the crisis moment of attempting suicide. But in those times when it seems that the action was compulsive, there is still the opportunity to intervene if we are aware of the risk. Being aware of circumstance raises our helper antenna to the risk before the compulsive act. People don't just wake up one morning with the sudden thought, I think I'll kill myself today. There is always a cause before the effect. Knowing this reality should ease the mind of the potential helper that is still uncertain that they could really help a person in need or that they would be caught off guard because they were not aware. You may not be the Guardian of the Golden Gate Bridge. You are just the ordinary person that happens to be in the right place at the right time, and I don't say that as a euphemism; it's true. The right place is not a bridge, it's a breakroom at work, a locker-room after practice, or a walk in the park on a sunny day. The right time is long before the means is in their hands, or even better, before they have considered the means and formulated a detailed plan. While I have had many harrowing moments that appeared to be compulsive, most of the interventions I have done were pre-emptive in nature. Someone was alert and called me or I was aware of the circumstances in a soldier's or teen's life that led to a conversation.

Compulsive suicide is a tragedy that can be stopped before it happens. Many survivors have often said, "If I could just go back in time, my friend would still be here." I have always loved movies that deal with time travel. In some ways I have felt like I have traveled through time whenever a person at risk says, "How did you know?" Knowing has nothing to do with being clairvoyant, but everything to do with being aware and able to read circumstances even when there are no signs.

I enjoy watching the show *Blue Bloods* with Tom Selleck as NYPD Commissioner, Frank Reagan. In one episode it appeared that he was going to be fired by the mayor. The commissioner told his personal assistant, "I'm tired, the kind of tired you can't sleep off." I've been there. Sergeant Kevin Briggs (the Guardian of the Golden Gate Bridge) has been there, as have many others that see bad things every week. In the movie *Field of Dreams*, Ray Kinsella, played by Kevin Costner, hears the voice of Shoeless Joe Jackson, "Ease his pain." When you lead a person to safety, you are easing their pain; they are not alone. And when you can help that person at risk before they get to the bridge, you are also *easing the tired* of the guardian that is out there every day fighting the battle to keep people alive. This morning, I will conduct the first workshop of the year in my hometown. I am so excited that 26 community members are joining us in the battle. I am once again encouraged that I'm not alone in what I do; they ease my pain. Eve Merriam penned "I dream of giving birth to a child who will one day ask, 'Mother, what was war?'" I dream of a day when a boy will ask his father, "Dad, what was suicide?" That day can come as more individuals learn how to lead those at risk to safety.

There will be times when those you help do have a well thought out plan. Again, I ask questions. "So, what do we need to do to make sure that you stay safe for now?" Often the person can tell me immediately, "I guess I need to give you my guns" or "I have a rope in the back of my car that I should probably give you." I always let them know if they give me the means that I will keep it secure and return it when they are no longer at risk. Protocol may require a different approach in a setting such as a school. Whatever the protocol, the goal is to help establish distance between the person at risk and their means. I was at drill in another state when a police officer from my hometown called. He was at the home of a man that had threatened suicide. The officer was able to secure the man's weapon, and they talked. The man assured the officer that he was better and wanted to know if he could have his weapon back. The officer wanted my opinion. My answer was no, not tonight. Secure it at the station and let the man know that he needs to see a counselor first. This should be standard procedure for anyone helping others. It is not a decision that an officer or a helper must make on their own.

In the leadership phase as throughout the model, we must be careful not to make promises that we can't keep. Even as I say this, there is a part of my brain that rebuttals. In a situation where the threat is imminent I have said whatever I needed to say to save the person's life, so do law enforcement personnel. But for the typical helper, when the threat is not imminent, and the means is not in hand, we want to be careful of making promises. Don't say, "I'll always be there for you," because it's not true. There are times when you can't be there. I always tell soldiers, "if you need me, call me. If I don't answer, call the crisis line." Unless you are the owner of the company and you can hire the person on the spot, don't say, "We'll get you another job." Making promises you can't keep can potentially put the person at an even higher risk as they ruminate on the thought that all people do is let them down.

Care for the caregiver is the final step in the Lead phase. Being part of helping a person to choose life is an incredibly rewarding experience, but it can also be a physically, emotionally, and even spiritually exhausting experience. We will talk in a later chapter about the importance of maintaining personal resilience. For now, understand that if you are going to lead others to renewed hope and improved resilience, you must be a practitioner of what you preach.

Lead Summary

- Leading addresses the how.
- How do you plan to end your life?
- How can we keep you safe for now?
- Who else have you told?
- What other resources do you have?

QUESTIONS

To be or not to be. That's not really a question.
Jean-Luc Godard

With every loss, survivors raise many questions. Sometimes there are no answers. In this chapter I simply wish to address a few of the most common questions that arise from workshop participants, many of which are survivors.

In 1978 Richard Seiden. Ph.D. professor at the University of California, Berkeley, conducted research to study the whereabouts of suicide attempters from the Golden Gate Bridge (GGB). His work was published under the title of Where Are They Now?[iii] in the winter 1978 volume of Suicide and Life-Threatening Behavior. His hope was to convenience Bridge Authorities to install suicide barriers that would deter potential jumpers. The authorities were convinced it would be a waste of money and that attempters would go to another bridge. His research proved them wrong.

The first known suicide from the GGB occurred within 90 days of its completion in May of 1937. In the first 40 years there were at least 625 suicides and perhaps hundreds more that we will never know about. Less than 1% of jumpers survive the fall. In recent years the annual number of losses has increased dramatically. Seiden's research showed that "the clear majority (94%) of GGB suicide attempters are still alive or died of natural causes." These were individuals that had been stopped, someone had intervened to keep them from jumping. They didn't go to another bridge. They discovered in their darkest moment on a literal Bridge of death that life was worth living.

Forty years after Seiden published his findings, the bridge district has announced plans to proceed with a suicide barrier on the GGB with a projected completion date of early 2021. Unfortunately, the hesitation on the part of those that could have made a difference sooner has cost thousands of lives. The future economic productive lost because at least 1600 people have died is estimated to be more than $2.2 billion. Fortunately, there have been many instances of people intervening on the bridge to keep others from jumping. One such person is Sgt. Kevin Briggs of the California Highway Patrol. He has rightfully earned the nickname of the *Guardian of the Golden Gate Bridge* for his intervention with as many as 200 attempters.

Does intervention save lives? Based on Seiden's research and a caring law enforcement officer, it most certainly does; my own experience is similar. So, if intervention saves lives, it makes sense that training individuals in intervention would save more lives by increasing awareness to the needs of those at risk and providing helpers with the skills to find nuggets of hope when it seemed all hope was gone.

Does asking the suicide question put the thought of suicide in a person's head; does it increase the risk? This is perhaps the question that is most often asked from workshop participants; and several studies have been conducted to address it. One such study entitled, *What's the Harm in Asking About Suicidal Ideation?* concludes, "Asking about thoughts of taking one's own life suggests that assessment is not associated with increases in suicidal ideation."[iv] In my experience, asking the suicide question is a liberating moment. The person at risk hears themselves responding to the question, and what made sense as the only option in the dark recesses of their mind when they were the only one who knew doesn't make as much sense when they hear the words coming from their mouth. Many times, after the crisis is averted I have heard the words, "I can't believe I was thinking of suicide." I liken it to a dream that seemed plausible, but upon waking, you realize that it didn't make sense at all. I recall a dream that I was singing my new song at the Country Music Awards, but when I woke and started singing the song in my dream it was rather silly, if not horrible. Our minds have an uncanny ability to rationalize the irrational. I am certainly no country music singer, although in my dreams my mind told me otherwise.

For several weeks as I pondered the possibility of suicide, it made sense in my mind that my family would be better off without me. The exclusion clause on a substantial life insurance policy had expired and I knew that my wife would receive the full benefit no matter my cause of death, even suicide. The wake-up call came for me when my son asked, "Dad, are you thinking about suicide?" In that moment, I understood that suicide was not the answer. I felt this huge weight had been lifted; I was not alone. My breathing got deeper and stronger, whereas for weeks it had been shallow. I was breathing in life. Amid the pain, emotionally, mentally, and even spiritually, I wanted to live.

The question is often raised, "Do you think my son or daughter, or dad really wanted to die?" I have often said in my workshops that I have never met anyone that really wanted to die. That statement gets some rather strange looks and even rebuttal. It is my belief that suicide is not the result of wanting to die so much as it is the result of not knowing how to live in the face of loss of some kind, be it the loss of a relationship, health, job, retirement account or anything else that brings meaning to life. The result is often an overwhelming hopelessness. Ultimately, hopelessness is in my opinion the greatest cause of suicide; it is also a primary characteristic of depression.

When we properly address the cause for suicidal thoughts, the thought of suicide often goes away. If the thought returns, we now have a previous history of coping that worked, and we grow stronger with each success. There is a great deal of truth in Friedrich Nietzsche's words, "That which does not kill us makes us stronger." One of the rebuttals I received came in the form of an email from a lady that heard my statement in a workshop. She wrote that at one point in her life she "did want to die", but then she goes on to share that she felt far from God and was in deep emotional pain. She gave two reasons why she wanted to die. When the emotional pain was addressed, and her questions of faith resolved, the thought of suicide vanished.

I often share with the person at risk that thoughts of suicide are much like any other thought. If we acted on every thought we had, all of us would be in jail. "I just want to die" or "everyone would be better off without me" are common thoughts for many people who may never reach the point of having a suicide plan. While hopelessness, pain or loss can take many forms, all the research indicates that 90% of suicidal ideation is caused by clinical depression or some other mental disorder. It is beyond the scope of this book or the lay helper to diagnose depression or mental disorder; we leave such matters to the trained professional. Our purpose is to provide first aid until the person at risk can get the further help they may require. The questions we raise in this section are provided to simply raise awareness.

A 14-year-old female confided that she was having suicidal thoughts. Two grandparents had died by suicide and she was concerned that she too would succumb. She asked if there was a suicide gene. She had obviously been doing some research, bringing up the Ernest Hemingway family. Hemingway's father, two siblings and a granddaughter died from suicide. Hemingway took his life in 1961. Researchers now claim that they have discovered a DNA marker that is present in individuals that have attempted suicide, but the same is true of heart disease and diabetes. The positive take away is that suicide is not inevitable, just as heart disease or diabetes is not. Perhaps the greater risk is not genes, but familiarity. The CDC reported in 2017 that the Cleveland, Ohio School District has the highest rate of suicide in the nation. Two in every ten students have attempted suicide; there is a tremendous amount of familiarity for every student. These individuals are related by familiarity, not blood. Add to this the extreme poverty which includes 4,000 homeless students and the risk increases further. The question for the teen that has lost family or the school that has lost students is, "What are you doing now to build a culture of health that reduces the risk of further losses?"

In a simulation exercise with a sheriff's department, I threw out every hook I could to get the deputy to ask the suicide question. Finally, I paused and immediately another deputy commented, "Why do we have to ask the suicide question? It was obvious the person was at risk." I responded, "Deputy, are you married?" He nodded, yes. "Did your wife ask you to marry her?" He nodded, NO. "Well then, how did you ever get married, because I know you didn't ask her." "OH, YES I DID!", he responded. "That's amazing! I would have thought that perhaps the two of you just showed up at the marriage chapel without ever discussing it just because it was obvious that marriage was the next step." The Deputy only half smiling said, "OK Chaplain, I get it. We have to ask the question."

We ask the suicide question to clarify that we are discussing suicide; this is one of those times where we absolutely need to be clear that we are talking about the same thing. It's interesting that in my workshops I will often have individuals raise the question, "How do you ask?" There is doubt in their voice that they could ever bring themselves to ask such a personal question. It does take courage to ask the suicide question the first time you do so. But again, I simply use the words, "Are you thinking of suicide?" At times I might preface it, "I am so sorry that you are having difficulty right now. Sometimes when people are going through things like you are going through, they have thoughts of suicide. Are you having thoughts of suicide?"

The follow up question from workshop participants is typically, "Do we have to use the word suicide?" No, you don't. You could say, "Are you thinking of killing yourself?" However, I never use the word harm, as in "Are you thinking of harming yourself?" The person thinking of suicide is not thinking of harming themselves; they are seeking to end pain, not create more. So, if we ask the question of harm, the person at risk could legitimately say no and you may think everything is fine when it is not. Similarly, I never ask,

"You're *NOT* thinking of suicide, are you? The Not, implies that I really don't want to hear the truth. The response will likely be, "Oh no, not me!"

LOCAL OUTREACH
TO SUICIDE SURVIVORS

Fayette County, Georgia is a community 25 miles south of Atlanta with a population of 111,000. In many ways it is typical of any town in the US. In three of the past six years it has had higher than national average suicide rates and two years of substantially lower rates.

Of the most recent 60 suicides in a five-year period, Mondays were the deadliest day of the week, accounting for 25% of the losses and Sunday was the lowest at 3%.

Males took their own lives at a rate of 3 to 1 over females and the highest rate for age category was 50 to 60 representing 28% of all loses; 15% of loses were under the age of 20.

In September of 2013, Dr. Frank Campbell invited me to a LOSS Teams Conference in Columbus, Ohio.

LOSS is an acronym for Local Outreach to Suicide Survivors. The concept is to provide local communities with a team of trained survivors who would go to the scenes of suicides to disseminate information about resources and be the installation of hope for the newly bereaved. After the conference, I came back to my hometown to establish the first LOSS Team in the state of Georgia. Dr. Campbell had warned that it may take time to build rapport with local law enforcement as we sought to embed the concept within our hometown and the law enforcement community.

In July of 2015, our break came when the city hired a new police chief. I had the opportunity to meet her at a community event and was encouraged to discover that she was also prior military. I presented the LOSS Team concept to Chief Janet Moon who welcomed the idea enthusiastically. Since that time the Fayette LOSS Team has been called upon several times. The first time being January 13, 2016 with the loss of the veteran, Kyle Lovett. Kyle took his life in his car at the busiest intersection in our town during the evening rush. Because of the very public loss, not only did the team serve his family, but we provided care over the next two weeks for more than 45 individuals that had been traumatized at the scene. The care that we were able to provide during this loss solidified the validity of the LOSS Team in our community.

Campbell's work with LOSS Teams is based on an Active Postvention Model (APM) and aligns with the work of Dr. Edwin Shneidman. In 1972, Shneidman developed the concept that postvention is prevention for the next generation. It is a concept that has governed Campbell's work for more than 30 years and provides motivation to the work we do today.

Survivors of suicide, those that have lost loved ones or friends to suicide, have an increased risk due to the familiarity. Additionally, as Campbell discovered in his original doctorial research, many survivors were not receiving counseling after the loss. Those that did eventually receive counseling did so on average 4.5 years after the loss. Through the Active Postvention Model utilized by the LOSS Team, the 4.5-year delay in seeking help was reduced to 39 days on average.

It should be noted that the LOSS Team does not provide on the spot counseling at the time of loss, but rather serves, as Campbell shares, as "a lighthouse pointing others to safe harbor." The *Listen Learn Lead* model would also have the lighthouse theme. Participants that take the L3 workshops learn about available resources that can be utilized to provide further assistance to those at risk. Individuals that participate on the Fayette LOSS team are required to learn the APM and the L3 model prior to joining the team.

I am grateful for the work of Dr. Campbell. Not only is he a pioneer in the field of suicide prevention and postvention, but he is a dear friend, encourager, and mentor. We were honored to host the first LOSS Team in Georgia in 2016 with individuals from seven states attending. No doubt, Dr. Campbell, as our keynote speaker was the reason for the tremendous response.

To learn more about Frank Campbell and the LOSS Team concept, visit their website at LOSSteam.com.

Through the LOSS Team, *Listen Learn Lead*, and other training opportunities, it is my personal goal to make my hometown the safest community in the state of Georgia, if not the nation. Currently, Georgia is ranked the 12th strongest. Over the past several years, New York and New Jersey have fought for first place in having the lowest rates of suicide in the nation. Both states have strong laws requiring mandatory training of certain professionals. New Jersey for example requires all public-school teachers and staff to receive 2 hours of training every year.

Many individuals of the 60 families that have experienced loss in our community over the past five years have participated in *Listen Learn Lead* training because of our being present with the LOSS Team when tragedy struck. They have accepted our recommendations to seek counseling in their grief, and they are learning ways to find hope in their new normal.

BEYOND SURVIVING
TO HOPE

I work with individuals every day that have lost hope. In their mind's eye, they see only death, divorce, difficulty, despair, darkness, or a myriad of other demons that zap one's ability to see a brighter future or any future at all. The Architect in the Matrix Trilogy said, "Hope, it is the quintessential human delusion." The philosopher, Friedrich Nietzsche, wrote at the age of 32, "In reality, hope is the worst of all evils, because it prolongs the torments of man." Interestingly, Nietzsche, at 44 years of age, was admitted to the Basel mental asylum where he remained until his death at 55. While some would deny the power of hope, through my own life experiences and being witness to the experiences of many others, I have discovered the incredible transforming power hope has to offer.

So, what is hope? Is it a human delusion and the worst of all evils as many believe? On the contrary, the enemy of hope is believing that things will never get better, that change is not possible - this is the true delusion. As Rebecca McGuire-Snieckus writes in *Hope, Optimism, and Delusion*, "Hopefulness and optimism are generally accepted by psychiatrists, psychologists, and the faith community as the preferred way of being."[v] Hope and optimism about the future has been identified in more than 90 studies as a vital key for recovery in mental illness and many other physical diseases.

The writer of Proverbs wrote, "Without vision, the people perish." It is hope that gives one vision, and the substance of that hope, according to the Bible, is faith. Those who argue that hope is a delusion would no doubt argue the same about faith. But we take many things on faith every day without recognizing it as faith. Driving down the road we have faith that the car headed our way will stay in its lane. We have faith that at the end of the month our employment check will be good when we cash it. Without a certain degree of faith, we wouldn't get out the bed in the morning; we would be frozen in fear and hopelessness. The writer of Hebrews tells us, "faith is the substance of things hoped for..."

Every great civilization, invention, achievement, family, and individual life is motivated by the hope that a better future will result because of the things we do. So perhaps a better question than trying to define what hope is, would be asking where is hope in what you are doing? Do you do the things that demonstrate hope?

Because what you do will either strengthen or diminish hope.

I was standing at the back of the formation of about 60 soldiers in the first visit to one of my Army units. The early morning sun was at our backs as the First Sergeant informed the unit that today was PHA (Physical Health Assessment) day. This is a day of getting shots, updating medical records and yes, answering the suicide question. The First Sergeant slid his sunglasses down his nose and winked as he said, "We all know how to answer the question, hooah?" It was an attempt at a covert message, that I recognized immediately. The First Sergeant was saying to the Soldiers, regardless of how you are really thinking, the answer is NO when you are asked if you are having or have recently had thoughts of suicide. In effect, he was sending a message to the soldiers that there was no hope for them, "Don't tell us how you really feel; deny it, or it will only make things worse." Before the formation was over I asked for a moment to provide a "Chaplain Word of the Day." Without pointing fingers or reprimanding the First Sergeant in front of his troops, I spoke on the importance of honestly facing the challenges of life. When we admit where we are instead of denying the struggle, we activate the mind to search for solutions, and our heart will thank us for being honest as stress hormones and blood pressure are reduced when we honestly admit challenges in our thinking. There is ample research that demonstrates that honesty really is the best policy, having positive effects on physical and mental health.

What I saw that day was that stigma is still very much present in the discussion of suicide. Soldiers are afraid if they speak the truth that they will lose their jobs or be singled out as unfit for deployment or other assignments. The same is true in the civilian world among teens and adults. They sense that if others knew what they were really thinking that they would be even further alienated by those that don't understand. The response of the helper can do much to reduce the stigma and greatly influence the installation of hope in the person at risk. However, many caregivers and those that are having thoughts of suicide often imagine the worst possible outcome. We have this image of a person being carried off under restraint and against their will to an asylum. Certainly, there are times when involuntary commitment is called for, however that is not the primary focus of the *Listen Learn Lead* model. If the person at risk is in an uncontrollable psychotic state, and they are unable to adequately address their own safety or there is a potential safety threat to others, call 911. However, *Listen Learn Lead* seeks to address the thoughts of suicide before the threat of loss is imminent.

Stats from my state's crisis line call center give evidence to the fact that hope can often be restored by simply having someone to talk to. Of the thousands of calls that are taken on the crisis line monthly, the clear majority never involve a 911 follow up. In the movie, *Castaway*, Tom Hanks played a FedEx employee stranded alone on a deserted tropical island for four years. An inanimate volleyball named Wilson was his only friend. After a storm, he thought he had lost Wilson and his hope plummeted. Often the way a helper best serves the person at risk is by simply being present and by listening. My dear friend, Frank Campbell, often uses the phrase, "installation of hope." It's a beautiful idea and the very thing which *Listen Learn Lead* seeks to do. Hope begins with listening.

Serving Soldiers in 40 states, I visit units where I have no office available or dedicated for my use. Often when a soldier comes to me I will ask if we can walk while we talk. Walking produces endorphin in the brain which reduces perception of pain. Walking also has a way of clearing the mind. It is amazing the number of times I have heard the words, "I am feeling better" or "I can see things differently now." Additionally, walking in sunlight increases the happy hormone, serotonin and helps the body to increase its production of vitamin D. Low levels of vitamin D have been associated with higher incidence of depression. Walking while talking has positive effects on mental and physical health.

While there are things we can do to help the person at risk rediscover hope, what can we do for survivors when the loss has happened and the loved one is gone? How does a family put the pieces together again when one of the pieces is missing? How do you respond to the words of well-meaning people whose trite platitudes only serve to stir up resentment, anger, and further feelings of loss? It was meant to be…everything happens for a reason…you're still young, there's plenty of eligible men out there…be thankful you still have two other children. These are just a few of the many comments that survivors have been told, and it hurts deeply. Unfortunately, some people don't know how to respond to those that grieve. It is beyond the scope of this book to address grief in detail; there are plenty of good books on grief that can help, but I do want to share a few thoughts.

"The new normal" is one of the most oft repeated phrases I hear from survivors. Things will never be the same; there is a void that can never be filled, even if one does remarry or have other children in which they can invest their lives. "But I am getting used to my new normal."

Be patient with yourself. Allow yourself to grieve, and don't put time constraints on what that process should look like. Find a caring competent counselor that can help you work through the grief process. That is the extent of my advice.

What I do want to address is this idea that everything happens for a reason. As a person of faith, I have heard this phrase all my life. The fact of the matter is, it is simply not true; it's bad theology. My son was not burned over 90% of his arms and half his face, so that I could file medical bankruptcy that would ultimately lead me to my own thoughts of suicide and now the work that I do in suicide intervention. Chad's accident was just that, an accident. God didn't cause the fire that hurt Chad to get my attention or to wake me up to my real purpose in life, even though today I cannot imagine doing anything else. The reason my son was hurt was because he did something he shouldn't have been doing near a fire. He threw a spray can of flammable liquid into an open flame and it caused a boiling liquid expanding vapor explosion (BLEVE).

Despite many challenges, I do believe in Romans 8:28 and this has been a great source of comfort to me over the years. While God didn't cause the explosion that hurt Chad, and He doesn't cause suicide, He did take that which had happened and made it work for my good. Some, would argue that it would have been good if my son had not been burned, it would have been good if there were no suicides. I agree, but then I am only a finite human being. Some may even question, how can you have faith that there is an all good and all-powerful God when there is so much suffering? Again, it is not the point of this book to argue the practical and existential problem of suffering. My point is this: I found a healthy way to work through my grief and pain, and I encourage you to do the same. I was not denying the pain was there, but I was no longer letting it dictate who I am. Grieve, YES, but do so in a way that will make you stronger. Don't be like the grieving father that resorted to a half a case of beer every night. That's not healthy; it only brings further destruction of life. Honor the memory of your loved one by choosing to live your life fully.

I carry in my heart a memory of the day Chad was injured, but it was one of thankfulness that he survived. But I also carry the memories of loved ones and friends that I have lost, because I wasn't there to help them. I no longer blame myself, but I do have the memory of loss. It is forever a part of me, and through that memory they live on compelling me to press on toward the City of Hope carrying as many as I can with me. When I am tempted to ball up in the fetal position and nurse my wounds, their memory is there reminding me of truth that is greater than the problems I will do battle with today.

Dr. Frank Page, in his book about his daughter, Melissa, shares that many survivors in the faith community often feel "tormented by the thought that some are using prayer request cover to make salacious sport over the loss. Many survivors picture themselves as leprous and out of favor with ordinary people and families.[vi] I am thankful for Dr. Page's candor and confess a degree of anger that such is ever the case within the church, but as Page says, it is ordinary people that do such things. So, I will continue to focus on hope and redemption.

Many survivors that I have worked with have expressed how they have felt incredible shame because of the loss. "If I..." is a common theme. "If I hadn't been so hard on my son. If I had only had the courage to ask...." Please do everything you can to walk away from such negative self-imposed shame and do not accept the shame that others may impose on you with talk about how you need to be more faithful now or you need to accept what God has done. Again, God doesn't cause suicide, and faith is a gift. Shame does not promote healing; it destroys. Forgiveness overcomes shame and restores hope. There is no future in shame, but only in hope.

Dr. Dale Archer, MD wrote in *Psychology Today*, "If I could find a way to package and dispense hope, I would have a pill more powerful than any antidepressant on the market. Hope, is often the only thing between man and the abyss. As long as a patient, individual or victim has hope, they can recover from anything and everything."[vii]

Two days after intervening for a soldier, I received a text. "I can see clearly now what you shared with me. Thanks for being there when I had lost hope." Did you catch that, "See clearly now?" Thoughts of suicide are confusing thoughts. I often tell those at risk, when we are confused, that is not the time to be making decisions about anything: whether you are buying a house or getting married and certainly when it comes to the question of life and death. Let's not make a permanent decision when we are confused. How about we stay safe for now, get a good night's rest and think through these things tomorrow?

Simply agreeing to and getting a good night of rest is a huge step toward life. It also helps to build resilience for a weary mind and body. Amazingly, many times the thoughts of suicide are gone altogether or greatly diminished, just like the clouds after a stormy night.

Surviving can become an all-consuming activity that drains the life out of the person trying to survive. Even the word *survivor* has a way of becoming our identity in a negative way. I realized in my own life I had to be more than a survivor. I had to be a thriver, an overcomer. I had to start doing things that would support a thriver mentality rather than a survivor mentality. Many others are doing the same, and it has changed the trajectory of their lives for the better. It is possible to move beyond surviving to restored hope. The journey is not an easy one but is a possible one. It can be a lonely journey, but there are many others on the journey too. We are not alone.

BROKEN SYSTEMS

In August of 2017, VA Secretary, Dr. David Shulkin, reported on the tragic and disturbing trend of veterans resorting to suicide on the grounds of VA facilities.[viii] In frustration and pain, many of these suicides are the result of being denied access to proper mental and physical care. Sadly, these brave individuals that willingly put their lives on the line in service to their country feel an incredible sense of betrayal. The system is broken.

It was a Friday night; I was prepping for two funeral services the next day. Both individuals had died naturally, one, an 85-year-old veteran and the other, a retired police officer that died of a heart attack. I received a call from one of our volunteers that a teen was in crisis. I asked her to call the Crisis Line. Half an hour later she sent me a picture of her phone showing that she had been on hold for 27 minutes. The crisis line had answered and immediately said, "Please Hold."

I immediately called her and got the address. In route, the police department called asking if I was available for the same person. Thankfully, tragedy was averted. But, once again we see that the system is broken. Those that are seeking to make a difference are wonderful, caring people. The crisis line counselor was doing her job the best she could, but it is within an underfunded and understaffed system.

According to the Suicide Prevention Resource Center (SPRC), "Every $1.00 spent on interventions that strengthened linkages among different care providers saved $2.50 in the cost of suicides." I was speaking with the executive director of a veteran nonprofit. He said, "I always feel like I am begging when I ask people or corporations to give." There was a time when I felt the same, but no longer. I was speaking at a breakfast gathering of one of our community's civic organizations; it was just three days after the loss of a teenage boy in our hometown. His death was the 15th suicide since the first of the year. I shared with the group, "I'm not here this morning to render tears. We need your support. You're not giving a handout. You are investing in your community!"

The typical suicide results in a $1.3 million economic loss. SPRC research reveals "more than 97% of this cost is due to lost productivity. The remaining 3% is associated with medical treatment, and 911 response." In my mind, this cost is born on the backs of the Waffle House waitress who will no longer get a tip from her favorite customer, the employer who must train a new employee, the church that will no longer receive a tithe from a faithful member, the political candidate that will not get a donation, the piano teacher who loses a student, the tire company that loses a lifelong customer…I could go on. In 2017, suicides in my hometown caused a $20 million economic loss; nationwide, the cost was nearly $100 billion. Then there is also the emotional cost on which we cannot put a figure, and we have not accounted for the economic loss from days lost from being out of work because the bereaved survivor could not bring themselves to get out of the bed and start their day.

As I was writing this chapter, I received an email that Washington State quarterback, Tyler Hilinski, had taken his life; he was 21. Currently, only 25 of the 129 Division 1 schools have full time mental health professionals on staff in their athletic departments, even though more than 1100 college students take their lives on college campuses every year, many of which are no doubt athletes. When the average salary of a Division 1 coach is $1.64 million, it would seem there is more that could be done to build safety on college campuses. The system is broken.

I learned a long time ago that I can't fix broken systems. I highlight the above to simply bring awareness to the reality of the way things are. While I can't overhaul broken systems, I can train individuals, and I can encourage communities and corporations and legislators to do what they can to help. An investment in suicide prevention is an investment in the community and the national culture of mental health. When we all support efforts to eradicate suicide, lives are saved, communities are stronger, and a vibrant culture of mental health begins to take shape.

Speaking of broken systems, I am reminded that *Bless the Broken Road* became the number one hit on the Billboard country music charts when Rascal Flatts recorded it in 2005. What some may not know is that it was written in 1994 and recorded by other artist prior to Flatts taking it to the top.

Every day I hear the stories of broken people. Many ruminate on past pains or catastrophize the future. In their present state they feel only pain. The pain is real and doing anything that invalidates the person's pain is not helpful, but I would be remiss as a Chaplain if I did not share that God can bless the broken road. Sometimes that is the only thing I know to say to those dealing with incredible pain be it emotional, physical, or otherwise. I pray that somehow knowing this can provide an instillation of hope in the darkness.

We can spend our days cursing the darkness and broken systems. We can be filled with resentment and envy that others have a life of ease or we can trust that God will bless the broken road that we find ourselves on. If a singer can take a song and make it a blessing to others in a way that others could not do with the same song, then we can choose to take the broken road we find ourselves on and allow it to be a blessing to others.

The next six chapters are simply personal reflections on ways that different components of community can possibly begin to make a difference.

LAW ENFORCEMENT COMMUNITY

It has been an honor to work with hundreds of law enforcement personnel (LEPs). Many work in agencies that are grossly underfunded and short on personnel. They are doing all they can to protect and serve the community. Thankfully, many are now receiving training called CIT through the National Alliance on Mental Illness (NAMI). The Crisis Intervention Team program is a model for community policing that brings together law enforcement, mental health providers, hospital emergency departments and individuals with mental illness and their families to improve responses to people in crisis. CIT programs enhance communication, identify mental health resources for assisting people in crisis and ensure that officers get the training and support that they need.

Hopefully, over time more officers will have the opportunity for training in CIT and even *Listen Learn Lead*, However, at present the percentage that have been trained is still single digits. In the summer of 2017, I had the opportunity of training more than 500 officers from three states in *Listen Learn Lead*. These were not rookies, but seasoned officers; three were retiring before the end of the year. Yet 95% had never had any training in suicide intervention. In the training of 36 Fire and EMS personnel in my hometown, only one had previous training while in the military. This is alarming in two ways. First Responders whether LEP or EMS are the ones that the public trusts to help when they make a 911 call. Yet many First Responders have stated that they feel ill equipped to handle such situations. Second, suicide within the ranks of First Responders is an innate risk that comes with wearing the uniform. While the military has done much to destigmatize the discussion of suicide, within the typical law enforcement agency, it is still a taboo subject. One officer confided that after a loss in their department, personnel were ordered not to go to the funeral and there was no honor guard for the officer that had ended his life. Little wonder that fellow officers had difficulty finding closure in the loss of their friend.

When I train law enforcement, I preface the class by letting attendees know that L3 is not a *hug a thug* class. There is standard of procedure that officers are mandated to follow, and I am not there to change their protocol or suggest that they ever allow themselves to be placed in an unsafe position when they are dealing with a criminal element. Safety is a given for everyone; safety first, not only for the person at risk, but also for the helper.

To maintain safety, LEPs often must make split second decisions that are later judged by the courts as to the appropriateness. As an example, in a potential suicide, would the use of a taser be considered reasonable or excessive force? It would depend on the circumstances. In 2013, a New Jersey man's life was saved because he was tazed by the officer when the man began to cut his own throat. The man was hospitalized for his self-injury, but the officer saved his life. There have been other cases where the outcome was not favorable. Unfortunately, society often criminalizes mental illness even though most individuals suffering from mental illness have no criminal intent. The dilemma for officers is trying to know the difference between those with intent on hurting others and those that are not. Often these are the cases that make the frontpage and the nightly news.

Unfortunately, there are some individuals that do use criminal intent to end their lives. Some of the first research into suicide by cop was completed by Sgt. Rick Parent of the Delta Police Department. Parent's research of 843 police shootings determined that about 50% were victim precipitated homicide. Police define victim precipitated homicide as "an incident in which an individual bent on self-destruction, engages in life threatening and criminal behavior to force law enforcement officers to kill them."[ix]

I have found it interesting how well officers trained in hostage negotiation resonate with the *Listen Learn Lead* model. The components are virtually identical. There is the need for active listening, building rapport, and showing empathy as they seek to influence individuals in a bad situation to a better outcome. The negotiator is concerned with keeping things calm and making sure that everyone is safe. They also seek to draw out what the person wants. "What kind of car/airplane do you need?" In the same way, there have been times when I have asked the suicidal person, "When was the last time you ate/ got a good night's sleep?" The person at risk of suicide is struggling to see the future. Many times, they haven't eaten or slept well in several days; food provides healthy mental fuel and sleep deprivation causes confusion. Often when the risk is mild and there is no plan or imminent danger of loss the helper can say, "Let's sleep on it. You don't have to make a decision today." It is amazing how often the thought dissipates with a night's sleep or a good meal. Other times the helper might ask, "If tomorrow was the perfect day what would it look like?" This is the miracle question used by coaches, therapists, and counselors to help a person envision a better tomorrow. When the person at risk can address this question, we often pinpoint what is causing the ideation, and at the same time help the person consider positive options. Failing these means there are times when calling 911 is necessary.

While law enforcement is trained in worse case scenarios, the civilian reading this section may be filled with fear that they would ever find themselves in such a difficult situation with a person on the proverbial bridge between life and death, but many officers would admit they have the same fears. The hope is that by knowing the risk and seeing the signs, the helper has the courage to intervene before the person at risk ever gets to the bridge.

Some officers like Sgt. Kevin Briggs, the Guardian of the Golden Gate Bridge operate in the crisis moment virtually every day. But again, the focus of *Listen Learn Lead* is intervention before the actual crisis moment ever occurs. Perhaps a better way of thinking of the model would be to call it Pre-crisis intervention; this is also the typical situation that law enforcement finds themselves in, not only with the public they serve but with those that they work with every day. Pre-crisis Intervention would recognize that suicide is an active thought before there is imminent threat of loss. By engaging in the model at the first sign of risk, we avoid escalation to an actual crisis moment.

There have been times when I have had to call for a health and welfare check on an individual that was too far away for me to get to. My concern in those times is, "Who will be sent; will they be able to render aid without escalating the problem?" Hopefully, the officer that is sent has been trained in CIT, but that is not always the case.

I had texted a soldier earlier in the day to check on her because she was not at the unit for weekend drill. I had been working through some issues with her for several months. I was just settling down in my hotel room to watch some football when I received a phone call. "Chaplain, I appreciate all you have tried to do for me, but I am going to kill myself." It's rare that someone would be that direct, but she seemed to have her mind made up. I asked her where she was. She said home. I asked for her address and within 15 minutes I was knocking on her apartment door, but there was no answer, the door was locked, and she did not answer her phone. I had no choice, but to call 911.

I heard the sirens as the soldier came from around the corner of the apartment building; she had been out walking. She stood in front of me, and I asked, "Do you hear the sirens?" She nodded, and I said, "They're coming for you." She began to cry. We went in her apartment, while my fellow chaplain waited to escort the officers in. I only had time to tell the soldier that everything would be all right, when two officers and three EMS personnel came through the door. Immediately without introduction or a moment of rapport building the conversation went as follows:

Officer in Charge (OIC): Are you _____? (asking the female her name. She nodded yes)

OIC: In a situation like this we have two options. You can come with me voluntarily or I can handcuff you and take you in the ambulance. (Soldier looked at me and began to cry. In my own mind, I was also somewhat alarmed at the abruptness and tone)

At this point, I introduced myself and I asked the soldier if she wanted to go to the hospital. She stated that she would rather have me help her. A conversation with the OIC followed for several minutes about what his protocol was in matters like this. I suggested he call his supervisor and explain the situation. After he got off the phone he said, "We're going to let Army take care of Army tonight, but if we get another call to come back, I have to do what I have to do." As they left, the second officer who had not spoken said, "Chaplain, thanks for being here for your solider tonight." He looked at the soldier and said, "Thank you for your service ma'am."

Law enforcement personnel have the arduous task of balancing service and safety. They are constantly in a state of vigilance, even when they are not in uniform. They live daily with the reality that if they are wrong, the consequences can be bad, very bad. However, in the incident above, safety issues were minimal. There was no weapon or immediate risk of harm. I am just guessing, but I suspect the OIC had never participated in a CIT training program. Law enforcement personnel are trained to move quickly to de-escalate potentially dangerous situations; however, there are times when moving slowly is the better choice.

After the officers left. I took a few minutes to build rapport with the solider. It may seem obvious that rapport was already in play, but we must always make sure. Then I asked, "So the thoughts of suicide were strong today?" With that we moved into learning. I was learning her *why* and she was learning once again that someone cared. I discovered that the reason that she had not been at drill was because she had just started a new civilian job. She needed to reschedule training with the unit but was told that she would be counted absent for today's missed drill. Her frustration with her circumstances had led to the thoughts of suicide. My fellow chaplain and I stayed with the soldier for about an hour. We talked about ways she could balance her civilian and army career. She is a person of faith, so we also talked about verses that she could meditate on to help bring peace to her mind. Once we felt assured of her safety, we departed.

To better serve the First Responder community, we established AFM911. You can learn more at AFM911.org. Through this program we teach the *Listen Learn Lead* curriculum in a format that is customized to the needs of law enforcement and Fire/EMS personnel. Our goal with this program is to build a culture of health within the First Responder community that strengthens those that serve and equips them to better serve the public. As Sgt. Brian Eden with Peachtree City Police Department said, "The skills learned through the workshops supplements what officers learn through the Crisis Intervention Training (CIT). Because of the efforts of AFM our officers are better equipped to recognize and respond to someone that is considering suicide."

Law Enforcement personnel often seem to walk a fine line simply because of who they are. Will their presence calm the situation or agitate it? I was standing by the sheriff at the graveside service of a teenager. I had tried on several occasions to bring the training to the church this deceased boy had attended. After the service, the pastor whom I know well, walked right past without speaking. The sheriff who was aware of the situation, saw my frustration. He said, "Ken, we are a lot alike." "How's that, Sheriff?" His answer was seared in my mind, "People don't want you till they need you, and when they need you, it is sometimes too late."

I would take the sheriff's comment a step further. A quick Google search of police response to mental health reveals a public perception that in such times not only do we not want you, but we don't need you. In a 2014 article on CityLab entitled *Think Twice Before Asking the Police to Deal with the Mentally Ill*" the author states, "What cops do is arrest people. If you don't want to be arrested, you probably shouldn't call the police."[x] In a more recent article, May 2017, entitled *Not Trained Not to Kill*", the author states, "In 34 states, training decisions are left to local agencies. Most, though, conduct no, or very little, de-escalation training. Chiefs cite cost, lack of staff, and a belief that the training isn't needed."[xi]

The seasoned veteran officer may have the belief that training is not needed. One officer was quoted as saying, "We learn by experience on the job". My question then would be, "How many people must die before we have enough experience to stop a suicide?" Training saves lives, sometimes that life is a fellow officer. According to the CDC, women in law enforcement have a higher rate of suicide than all other careers. Recognizing this perception that some officers have that training is not needed, I come back to my main goal in working with law enforcement in the first place. It is the same goal that I have in working with the military, and that is to eradicate suicide within the ranks of those that serve. The secondary benefit for law enforcement is that in learning skills to keep their partner safe, they also learn skills that can be used with the public. *Listen Learn Lead* is simply another tool for the toolbelt.

I was called to teach a workshop in a police department after the suicides of two of their officers within a six-month period. At the start of the workshop I polled the participants, "Who was *voluntold* to be here today?" Half the class raised their hands. Throughout the day the emotion of many was evident. At lunch with one of the officers, he said, "I wish I had this training 20 years ago; five of my friends might still be alive today." At the end of the day on our exit survey we ask the question, "Knowing what you now know, if you had not been told to be present for this class would you come?" 100% of the participants said YES. A nearly similar response has been true of the more than 10,000 civilians that have attended. The few that have said no, or I am not sure, added their reasons. "It was too close to home" or "I don't know if I am emotionally strong enough to do this."

The truth is, First Responders, as they are called, are not the real first responders. They are second responders, and they know it. Regardless of the emergency, the real first responders are not the ones that wear the uniform. The ordinary individuals that make the call or do the CPR or see the accident happen at the intersection are the true first responders. When it comes to suicide intervention, it is the ordinary citizen that sees the signs and has opportunity to intervene. It's the mother that knows her child is being bullied; it's the coworker during lunch that can see his friend is isolating himself; it's the coach on the ballfield that knows his team member is struggling. These are the real first responders. We are not asking everyone that takes our workshops to leave their current jobs to pursue intervention as a full-time career. We simply want to equip ordinary people to be prepared when the crisis arises. Knowing what to do in the difficult situation can be the difference between life and death. One way or another, training saves lives!

Some of the best workshops I have conducted have brought together both law enforcement and the communities they serve. When Sheriffs and Chiefs encourage community involvement in the training, it creates a synergistic effect and a *"We're in this together"* approach to eradicating this epidemic that takes twice as many lives every year as homicide. One sheriff's deputy was grateful for the opportunity to be in the same class with civilians saying, "Being together with the community we serve was good for all of us. It helped me to see things from their perspective, and I think it helped some to understand that I am a human being too."

SCHOOL COMMUNITY

Recently I was visiting with a friend that told me of a situation she had been involved in. A teenage girl was asked to go to the prom. She was so excited as this would be her first time out with a young man. Her mother went shopping with her to pick out a dress. She had her hair and nails done for the special occasion and the evening of the prom arrived. But her date never showed, nor did he answer her calls. On Monday at school she discovered that she was the victim of a cruel joke. The boy never intended to go to the prom with her.

I posted this scenario on Facebook, curious as to how others would respond. One father said, "I would be in jail!" Another said, "I would be having a serious talk with the boy and his parents." Other comments included the boy was a psychopath, I would send him the bill for the girl's expenses and the emotional trauma. Others said, "I would pray for her" or "bless her heart." How would you respond?

Looking at the responses, it was clear that 90% were focused on the boy, what they would say or do to him. Little attention was given to what the response would be with the young lady, but I can imagine. Some would say, "There are plenty of fish in the pond...Be glad he didn't show up...You don't need someone like him in your life..." All very true responses but known which would validate the present pain of being the brunt of an evil joke. What would you say that might address the mental anguish she was experiencing? Is it possible that such an experience could lead to thoughts of suicide? The fact is many similar experiences do for teens every day all across the country.

Pike County, Georgia is a rural community one hour south of Atlanta. The most recent 10-year suicide rate has been 50% higher than the national average. Of the 17,000 residents within the community, 3,400 are students from pre-K to 12th grade. In 2014, the community had experienced the third suicide of a teen in a five-year period. Shortly thereafter, Superintendent, Dr. Mike Duncan, through collaboration with Pike County Family Connections, had our team begin a training series for his teachers; this was a full year prior to the state mandated annual training of certified school personnel through the Jason Flatt Act.

As part of the Intervene Challenge, we began with the two-day Applied Suicide Intervention Skills Training (ASIST) workshop for all school counselors. To best facilitate broad coverage to all faculty we produced a video based on the *Listen Learn Lead* curriculum that was distributed through the school intranet; and have returned every year for in-class workshops in *Listen Learn Lead*. As of the writing of this book, there have been no suicides in the school system since implementation of the training. Says Duncan, "It is not hyperbole when I say the Intervene Challenge is the most impactful professional learning I have encountered in my 20-year career. I left the training a different person, equipped with the skills to save a life. I now recommend this training to everyone." Training saves teens!

My first memory of suicide did not occur until my second year of college when a childhood friend's dad took his life. High school kids today seem to deal with so much more. According to the Jason Foundation and the CDC, suicide is the SECOND leading cause of death for college-age youth and ages 12-18. More teenagers and young adults die from suicide than from cancer, heart disease, AIDS, birth defects, stroke, pneumonia, influenza, and lung disease, COMBINED. Each day in our nation, there are an average of over 3,470 attempts by young people grades 9-12.

Unfortunately, many school systems are perplexed as to how to respond when a loss does occur. The American Foundation for Suicide Prevention, in collaboration with the Suicide Prevention Resource Center, provides an excellent resource entitled, *After Suicide: A Toolkit for Schools*. In this document, administrators, counselors, and faculty will find meaningful ways to respond to crisis, how to help students cope, and discussion on various other aspects of postvention care. Of note, it is suggested that, "if there appears to be contagion, school administrators should consider taking additional steps beyond the basic crisis response, including stepping up efforts to identify other students who may be at heightened risk of suicide, collaborating with community partners in coordinated suicide prevention effort, and possibly bringing in outside experts."[xii]

Suicide of a friend, is a memory that never goes away. Recently I was having lunch with my friend, Ed. We had not seen each other since high school, some 30+ years ago. As I shared with Ed what I do, I sensed that something was on his mind. "Ken, do you remember Jim?" He was a student that we had befriended to keep the bullies at bay. I had graduated a year before Ed and Jim. "Sure, I remember Jim. How's he doing?" Ed paused for a moment, "He took his life the year after you graduated." Ed went on to share that on a Friday, after school, Jim wanted to know if they could get together during the weekend. Ed told him he would be busy. The following Monday Ed discovered that Jim had taken his life. Tears formed in Ed's eyes as he pondered, "I have wondered through the years if he would still be alive if I had only been available as his friend that weekend." Suicide of a friend or loved one is a heavy burden for anyone to carry for a lifetime; but there are thousands like Ed that do.

We can't change what has happened, but we can't carry the burden all our lives of *what if,* either. For some reason, a few specific lines from the Soldier's Creed comes to mind. "I will never accept defeat. I will never quit. I will never leave a fallen comrade." I know that I can't stop wars and I can't keep all soldiers from dying on the battlefield in the desert or on the home front from the battles in their own mind; all I can do is what I can do. The same is true of you, but you can do more than you perhaps may realize. The Creed continues, "I am disciplined, physically and mentally tough, trained and proficient in my warrior tasks and drills...I stand ready to deploy and engage...I am a guardian of freedom...I am an American Soldier."

When I was in school it was all about reading, writing, and arithmetic. School was the place of education; many today have become war zones. Now students must learn how to stay alive when there is an active shooter, how to avoid sex trafficking and things I never knew about in school; suicide is one of them. It's time for the school community to educate students on how to stay alive and help their friends do the same when it comes to thoughts of suicide. There's a war on the home front, and schools have become a battlefield.

For teens we have created two wrist bands. One is green, representative of leading and life and simply says I WILL INTERVENE. The other is yellow, representative of listening and says, WHAT QUESTION? We created a specific website at WhatQuestion.org and a brief video to help raise awareness and remind us to ask the all-important question, "Are you having thoughts of suicide?" When teens are willing to ask their friends the suicide question, they can save lives.

We also encourage teens to tell an adult that can help. In the military we have a saying for security, "If you see something, say something." The same holds true for teens. The friend at risk may say, "Don't tell anyone what I have confided in you." Potential suicide of a friend is a confidence a teen cannot keep. It doesn't matter if the hurting individual threatens that the friendship will be over if they tell. The truth is, the friendship will be over if they don't.

Speaking for myself, I knew that somehow, I had to transform the burden I carry for those that are hurting or have died. I had to turn the darkness into light for my own sake and the sake of others. I did so through a disciplined effort to learn the skills of intervention and the courage to be ready, willing, and able to help, ready to deploy to those in need. Because of the training, I can engage those at risk in their darkest hour and help restore hope that sets them free. The burden is always there, but it has been transformed into a purpose to save the ones I can.

Schools need to continue exploring ways to improve the process by which they seek to address the issues of suicide. There is much room for improvement. Some policies need to change. If policy is more important than people, we will continue to struggle with the culture of community mental health. On a Tuesday following an intervention with a ninth-grade boy four days earlier, I received a text message from him.

Hey, is it possible for you to get child protection services off my butt? Please make them stop because now I'm being sent to a mental hospital. I'm OK but this is going to make things worse.

Someone had sent his suicide note to the school counselor who then called the Department of Family and Children's Services. There is a place for involuntary commitment, but this was not one of them. In another conversation, a teacher shared that she wanted to help a student she knew was suicidal, but policy required that if suicidal thought is known or suspected, the student must be immediately escorted to the counseling office without further discussion between the student and the teacher.

Many policies that are implemented are done so to reduce the possibility of litigation; no one wants a law suit. But it's rather disturbing that a student feels that he cannot confide in a trusted teacher without the immediate response being, "I can't talk about this, I have to take you to the counselor now."

Many of the challenges that the school system experiences are also seen in the medical community.

MEDICAL COMMUNITY

On several occasions in our workshops, the question has been asked, "Will the person at risk answer truthfully if the direct question of suicide is raised?" I find it interesting that the question is most often raised by individuals within the mental health and medical community. My short answer is, "They may not, particularly in a clinical or medical setting." The soldier that must answer the question on Physical Health Assessment Day with his unit may say NO when the real answer is YES. It's also true of the police officer that is fearful that he may have his weapon taken away and be assigned to admin duties, or the high school student who is asked by the school counselor who got a tip from a student that had already had their friend tell them they were suicidal.

I was present when a 14-year-old said no to the police officer because his mother was standing beside him, even though the officer had in his hand a printout of the text the boy had sent a friend, a suicide good bye note.

From my own experience, I said, "NO" even as I was making application to go back in the military in the hope that I would be deployed and killed by the enemy. However, a year later when my son asked me the question I said, "YES". I also said, "Yes, I had" to the doctor a month later when I discovered that my adrenal system had crashed, and my cortisol levels were constantly elevated.

We must consider the context and the environment in which the question is asked. The clinical or medical setting for many people is cold and impersonal. When a soldier is *next in line* and the question is immediately put to them by a clinician checking boxes on an intake form, it is easy to say no. The reason I said yes to my doctor was because I was seeing her to find additional help after my son had encouraged me to do so. Furthermore, this doctor was amazing. When she discovered that I was a soldier, she told me that she had been too, at Ft. Sam Houston. When I told her what I did and that I had previously had thoughts of suicide, she told her PA to take all her other patients, and for the next 90 minutes we talked. Never have I felt such acceptance and care from a physician. I don't recall when any other physician had ever spent more than 10 minutes in the room with me.

The American Association of Suicidology published the results of US and Canadian studies in *Comparison of the Effects of Telephone Suicide Prevention Help by Volunteers and Professional Paid Staff*. Research since the 1960s has consistently found that lay volunteers are better at helping suicidal callers than professionals. Yet, professional degrees are increasingly becoming requirements for helpline workers. We conclude from these results and the consistent pattern of findings in previous research that there is no justification for requiring that suicide prevention helpline workers be mental health professionals. In fact, the evidence to date indicates that professionals may very well be less helpful and effective on the telephone with suicidal individuals and people in crisis, when compared to trained lay volunteers.[xiii]

The *Listen Learn Lead* model emphasizes the importance of building rapport before asking such an intimate question about life and death. In the clinical and medical setting, time constraints and full waiting rooms don't allow for much rapport building. However, just a small amount of rapport can go a long way, and as we have already discussed, rapport can be built much more quickly than most people believe possible.

Several studies have been conducted on the high rate of infant death in some orphanages. The phenomenon is now known as *failure to thrive*. As Maia Szalavitz points out in a 2010 article in *Psychology Today*, "Babies who are not held and nuzzled and hugged enough will literally stop growing and-if the situation lasts long enough, even if they are receiving proper nutrition-die." In my opinion, this is analogous to what often happens in the clinical setting or the school system. We have a policy (nutrition) and we think that is enough. While the Department of Education has issued a "No touch" policy to avoid litigation and any questions of impropriety, we fail to recognize that through empathy we can touch the heart and mind.

Suicide is the 2nd leading cause of death among teens and the 10th leading cause of death in the US, yet there is very little, if any, training within the medical community to address this epidemic. There will always be some at risk that will say no regardless of the care we take in asking the question. However, what I have seen nearly a thousand times is that people want to tell the truth.

What I often share with law enforcement is applicable to medical professionals as well. There is a difference between an interview room and interrogation room. Interview rooms are typically outside of lock up for the sake of the witnesses or victims that are being interviewed. While interrogation rooms are usually within secure areas to question suspects in a crime. One of the reasons we encourage helpers not to use the word "commit" when asking the suicide question is to move away from any idea that criminalizes mental illness. When individuals feel like they are being interrogated we can expect the answer to be no. But when we take time to build rapport and a safe caring environment, the truth comes out.

I will add that there have been times when the initial response to the question is no, but I will come back to the question a few moments later, in the form of an interrogative statement – "Tell me about your thoughts of suicide." My insurance agent was concerned about a friend and was asking for advice on how to help him.

He asked, "What if he says no?" I encouraged him to ask in the form of a statement. He was surprised, "Wow, that's what we do in the insurance business." I was puzzled. He went on to explain, "When I take an application for car insurance, I ask the proposed insured to tell me about his last three traffic citations. We learned in a sales class that if we ask, 'Have you had any tickets in the past three years?' that we get a lot of no responses. But the response is different when we say, 'Tell me about your last three tickets.' It's as if the person knows that we know that they are not perfect drivers." WOW, such a powerful parallel. When we ask the suicide question or put it in an interrogative statement it lets the person know that it's OK to talk about it.

CORPORATE COMMUNITY

A headline in the Atlantic Press read, *Workplace Suicides Are on the Rise*. One recent study found that the global recession that began in 2007 could be linked with more than 10,000 suicides across North America and Europe.[xiv] Corporate America can do much to address the issue of suicide. Organizations that offer training in intervention demonstrate care for their employees. Caring makes good business sense. In my former career as a real estate broker, we provided our staff with access to chaplain support. The care that we demonstrated instilled loyalty and commitment with the team and exceptionally low turnover.

One of our workshop participants was sent by his employer, a large government contractor. He shared verbatim with me a conversation that took place within just a few weeks of attending the training. (the names have been changed)

Cindy had just returned to work after being gone for a month due to the loss of her husband and child in a boating accident. They were buried in their hometown in the Midwest. Cindy has no family living within 300 miles. She was sitting at her desk despondent, mulling through a pile of papers, trying to get caught up. When Steve walked in and had the following conversation.

Steve: Hi Cindy. We're glad to have you back...we missed you.

Cindy: Thanks. (very pensive deep in thought)

Steve: Listen, I want you to know how sorry we all are about the loss. I wanted to be at the funeral, but the Dubai contract had to be settled.

Cindy: That's OK Steve.

Steve: If there is anything I can do to help you get caught up I am here for you. (Cindy nods without saying a word)

[Steve walked out of her office not sure if he should have asked the question. Two days later, in the company breakroom, he did.]

Steve: We would love for you to rejoin us at our Wednesday lunch outing.

Cindy: I'm sorry Steve, I just know I...I wouldn't be much fun, and I don't want to bring others down.

Steve: Are you eating well when you get home at night?

Cindy: I nibble…just haven't wanted to do much of anything.

Steve: How well are you resting at night?

Cindy: I don't…I toss and turn all night and then I come to work and can't seem to focus… EVERYTHING is confusing. (Tearful) My husband is gone. My precious little Tyler is gone…. I don't want to be here. (choking up)

Steve: Cindy I know you have been through so much. I can't even imagine the pain you must be feeling. (Pausing) Have you talked with anyone about your loss?

Cindy: Just you…Every time I call John's mom she cries…I have tried everything to comfort her, but nothing helps.

Steve: I know it is difficult for her too. It's not natural to lose a son and a grandchild…But I am concerned for you. (Cindy looking down, Steve pausing for a moment) You don't want to be here? (inquisitive) What do you mean?

Cindy: (Still looking down) Nothing really matters anymore. Work doesn't mean anything without a family to come home to at night. Without them, life doesn't really matter.

Steve: Cindy with all that has happened and based on what I hear you saying, I wonder…. Are you thinking of suicide? (Cindy raises her head and looks eye to eye at Steve)

Cindy: Would it be such a bad thing if I was?

Steve: So, you have had thoughts of suicide?

(Cindy nods and looks away)

Steve: Do you have a plan?

Cindy: A plan?

Steve: Do you have a plan as to how you would end your life?

Cindy: Well you know, John was a hunter...he taught me how to use his guns....

Steve: Have you thought about when you would do this?

Cindy: The 14th has crossed my mind.

Steve: The 14th?

Cindy: Yes, the 14th of next month.... that was our anniversary day....

Steve: You said a moment ago that everything is confusing. You know me; I don't ever make decisions about anything till I am clear on things; and I don't want you to make a life and death decision in a state of confusion.... Cindy, I don't want you to end your life. What can we do to get you to a better place?

Cindy: I'm not sure....

Steve: How about I call Karen. You met her last year at our July 4th party. She is a counselor at our church. I will call and see if she can meet us at the office. Then she can go with us to your house.

Cindy: My house?

Steve: Yes, we need to do some things to keep you safe for now. I would like to keep John's guns at my house while we figure out the next step, OK?

Cindy: OK...

Steve: Cindy, you need to know that the thoughts you are having are normal. You have been through so much, but I also know that there is a part of you that wants to live.

Cindy: How do you know that?

Steve: Well, I am just guessing at this point, but I can't help but think that if it was John that was sitting here, and you were gone, you would want John to keep living... Am I right?

Cindy: (slight smile for the first time) Without question!

Steve: That's what I thought. So, let's do the same for you that you would want John to do for himself if he were here.

Cindy: Thanks Steve...

Steve did a beautiful job of working through the model. He demonstrated care, he built rapport, he showed empathy. He then asked the suicide question and moved into the leading phase by asking if Cindy had a plan and when she planned to do this. He also used the very words I have used with others to help them find reasons to live. The corporation that sent Steve to the training is to be commended. They understand the benefits of building a culture of health, and they are a stronger organization because of their willingness to engage in building the culture.

VETERAN COMMUNITY

During World War II, three years after the Bataan Death March, Lt Colonel Henry Mucci led the 6th Ranger Battalion in the raid of a prison camp at Cabanatuan in the Philippines. His mission was to save the lives of the 500 remaining POWs held there by enemy forces. The Cabanatuan mission is remembered today as the Great Raid and the most successful extraction of Prisoners of War in history. Many of those prisoners spent their days filled with hopelessness and despair that they had been forsaken. When liberation finally came, many hid in their huts in fear that it was a trick of the enemy to kill them.

Although I am an Army Chaplain, I am not an American hero, but I often find myself working with those who are; many of them are broken. They have lost their way and their identity. They no longer see themselves as warriors. Some never seek help because of the erroneous belief that real warriors never express emotion, and certainly don't ask for help.

The second of three generations of Marines called me to work through some painful thoughts he was having. His son, a third generation Marine had taken his life. The grandfather, a first-generation Marine refused to attend his grandson's memorial service, saying, "Real Marines don't take their life." Two years later the elderly grandfather died. All the emotion and anger that the caller had experienced when his son took his life came flooding back when he stood at the graveside of his father saying, "You couldn't be here for your grandson, but I am here for you." As he shared the pain, it was evident that heroes are humans too. They bleed like all people do, and though they do the best they can to present themselves as men or women of steel, they are in the end human beings.

As a Chaplain I learned the ethics and rules of war. One of the rules that every officer and NCO is familiar with is to strike the enemies' weakness; it is also true that we must know our own. Nations, for security purposes, don't broadcast their weaknesses to others; that would not be prudent. But individuals often do the same, and the stigma that continues to surround the discussion of mental illness is evidence of this fact. An ancient text reminds me that, "When I am weak, then I am strong." I must know where I am and not deny it, if I want to ever get to where I really want to be. Denying reality puts us in a never-ending flight mode always fleeing from our present circumstances but never arriving anywhere. We must conquer the battle within our own minds, but often doing so is our greatest challenge. We may have earned ribbons and be highly decorated for courage and valor in the desert or the jungle, but now we must exhibit the same courage on the home front with this battle in the mind.

Because of my work with Armed Forces Mission, many of the interventions I have conducted have been with Veterans. Veterans represent a disproportional number of the suicides that occur every day in the US. I was in a conversation with a Hollywood actor that is also a Marine Veteran. He wanted to know if our organization, Armed Forces Mission was "just another bleeding-heart organization looking for a sob story and a handout". I assured him that we weren't. At the same time, I am cognizant of the fact that there is an element of society today that perpetuates a sense of brokenness and entitlement, and unfortunately, this is true to a degree in the military and veteran community. It angered me when one of my son's friends claimed to have PTSD because of Navy Basic Training and was medically discharged with a monthly government check. As my Hollywood friend said, "Regardless of training and indoctrination, people who enter military service ultimately are products of the society they volunteered to defend."

At Armed Forces Mission, we are Veteran led, and we operate from the position of strength. We are leaders serving our community for the benefit of all. Many of my chaplain pep talks are with leadership frustrated with the military becoming a social experiment and having to deal with soldiers that should not be soldiers.

At the same time, PTSD is real, and the rewiring of neurons from trauma can impact one's ability to properly function in society. Regardless of who should or should not be in the military, the system is stuck in the mode of *management of,* rather than *solutions to* crisis and the problem is self-perpetuating. Our goal at Armed Forces Mission is to overcome brokenness, not keep people stuck in it. We are not trying to build recurring streams of income on the backs of hurting people. When we work with Veterans, we immerse them in an environment that instills hope and a vision for the future because we hold to what the Good Book says, "Without a vision, people perish"; as a result, we see lives transformed.

Many people, not just veterans, live in desperation because they have never learned to think about how they think, especially after traumatic events have impaired their ability to think. There is no formal learning in school on how to face crisis. We, as humans, are rather reactive by nature. We attempt the best we can to manage chaos and crisis when it comes but do little to train for it in advance.

One of the deficiencies of some Veteran support programs is the lack of the spiritual component even though the empirical findings have identified spirituality as a tremendously useful health resource. The Combat Trauma Healing Manual by Chris Adsit is a resource that we use regularly in support groups for veterans. Through 10-week group meetings we have seen shattered lives restored and veterans empowered to help other veterans. One of the keys is the ability to accept God's grace.

Every night a veteran would secure his perimeter at the apartment where he lived; it was rather unsettling to the other residents. His wife told me that the girls keep him up at night. When I responded, "I didn't know you had children?" she said, "We don't. It is the two little girls that were killed when he was ordered to fire on a car that was headed toward their convoy at a high rate of speed late at night." Eventually, the veteran ended up in jail. When I went to get him out, the judge said, "Ken, this is the second time he has been here. I can't keep showing him grace." In the parking lot of the jail I asked the veteran if he had heard the judge. He responded, "Yes Sir, I did. But I don't deserve grace anyway." On one hand, the veteran is correct, but that is the whole point. Grace is something we don't deserve; that's why it is called grace. Grace is the unmerited favor of God, that we are loved and accepted no matter what we have done in war.

In his state of hypervigilance, the veteran would oscillate between increased anxiety and total exhaustion. When he slept, it was never restful but always nightmares. Such is the case for many veterans diagnosed with PTSD. Adding to the pain is the belief held by many within the mental health and medical community that there is no cure for PTSD. No cure, Really? Is this the message we want to convey? Little wonder with such a prognosis we see a suicide rate among veterans 200 to 300% higher than the public.

When we say, "There's no cure", we are saying there is no relief of symptoms from the condition, there is no possibility of becoming sound or healthy again; we're just managing chaos rather than overcoming it. Is there a cure for PTSD? Some say, no, but I answer with a resounding YES. A person suffering with PTSD can find relief that is life enhancing (suicide does not have to be the answer). There is the possibility of renewed resilience which restores the individual to sound health and a life of hope and joy.

Over thirty years ago, my father was diagnosed with Lymphoma; at the time there was no cure; he died at 53. Because of breakthrough research, this once fatal diagnosis is now curable. Regarding PTSD, I have seen this truth in my own life and the lives of thousands of veterans that transformation is possible. Those who want to insist that there is no cure for PTSD need to keep doing their research until they find the cure. The position that there is no cure perpetuates hopelessness. Building new healthy synaptic bridges does take time, but it is possible. Those who are working to find a cure, would agree, we have only just begun to understand the ability of the brain to form synaptic connections that are helpful following a traumatic event that has jumbled the wiring. The mind has an incredible ability to heal itself.

I would be remiss as a chaplain if I did not recognize the power of God to transform the mind. The ancient text that we call the Bible is an incredible resource that is rarely considered in a world of free thinkers. Nevertheless, I have experienced healing within my own mind and witnessed such healing in countless others. When considering your options for PTSD treatment, don't overlook the spiritual component. It is, after all, a place where millions throughout time have found the cure.

Do you still see yourself as a warrior? It's a question I have asked many veterans. Unfortunately, some say no. They have taken on the identity of brokenness, but brokenness is not an identity; it is a condition and one that can change. Exodus 15:3, says, "The Lord is a Warrior", it is part of God's identity; it is part of your identity too. I have a sneaking suspicion that God looks upon you with particular favor because you are a warrior. After all, He is too.

Thankfully, there is a movement to drop the D from PTSD. I am in agreement with Retired U.S. Army General Peter Chiarelli, director of the organization One Mind, "Drop the D, that word is a dirty word. The use of PTSD suggests the ailment is pre-existing, when in reality, it is a predictable reaction to combat stress."

I would also add that suicide is just a thought and one that is normal in abnormal situations. There are many contrary thoughts that we have every day that we do not act upon. Suicide should be one of those thoughts that we can talk about without having to act upon it.

If you are having thoughts of suicide tell someone. Tell a battle buddy, call the national Lifeline at 1-800-273-TALK or contact me. Taking the step to tell others is a courageous step in the right direction.

Faith Community

The Faith community is not exempt from the devastation suicide brings. A LifeWay study found "three-quarters (76 percent) of churchgoers say suicide is a problem that needs to be addressed in their community. About a third (32 percent) say a close acquaintance or family member has died by suicide."

In exit surveys from our workshops, 100% of the pastors responded that they received no suicide intervention training in their seminary education. One had taken a suicide workshop as a psychology major in his undergraduate degree. Neither of my alma maters for my Master of Divinity in 1990 or my Doctorate in Counseling in 2005 offered any discussion of suicide prevention. Two other challenging responses from the Lifeway Research revealed, "more than half (55 percent) of churchgoers felt people in their community are more likely to gossip about a suicide than to help a victim's family, and only 12% of churchgoers say their church has a crisis response team."

As a person of faith, I am thankful for many churches that have taken a lead in providing training for their members and the community, but I am grieved by the number that haven't, and some that even seem to be adamantly opposed to the idea. Tabernacle in Carrollton, Georgia is one of the champions. In 2017 they hosted four workshops for the community. Members attended as did school counselors, law enforcement and others. The church leadership has demonstrated that suicide is a matter that they feel obligated to address, and it is making a difference, lives are being saved. First Baptist in Fayetteville, Georgia is another strong advocate. They have supported the mission since inception and hosted two to three workshops every year since 2013, with individuals from seven states attending the inaugural state LOSS Teams Conference in 2016.

Lady, if you mention God one more time...

In addition to *Listen Learn Lead*, I teach a two-day workshop called Applied Suicide Intervention Skills Training (ASIST). ASIST is a world class curriculum with more than one million care givers trained over the past 30 years. On day two of the workshop we do a bridge simulation exercise. In every instance the training calls for several participants to attempt to talk the person down and eventually someone always does. However, there was one occasion when the opposite happened. The conversation went as so...

Helper: What are you doing up there?

Person at risk (PAR): Why would you care?

Helper: Because God loves you...

PAR: Uh

Helper: There's nothing too big for God...

PAR: Lady, if you mention God one more time I swear I will jump!

Helper: But God...

The person at risk jumped and the helper teared up as she came to the realization of what had happened. Thankfully, it was only a simulation. To my friends at Livingworks that license me to teach the ASIST workshop, I beg your forgiveness for not following standard procedure, but the conversation that followed was well worth the deviation.

Now, before I am accused of having a low view of scripture, let me just share that I happen to believe that there is a place for faith and scripture in working with those at risk. I also happen to have a strong belief in 2 Timothy 3:16 that scripture is useful for teaching, for showing mistakes, for correcting, and for training character. But I also believe that many times well-meaning individuals can accidently use the scripture in the same way a deranged prisoner might use a sharp instrument as a shank. A skilled surgeon, on the other hand, would use a sharp instrument such as a scalpel to save lives.

Believe me, I always pray and ask God to give me wisdom in what I say as I enter an intervention. But I am also always careful in navigating any discussion of faith, not that I avoid it, but I am careful. Research by LifeWay suggests that, "About a third of suicide victims (35%) attended church at least monthly during the months prior to death, according to their friends and family." So, there is some indication that many suicide victims were considering matters of faith before they died. They were searching for answers, for hope, for purpose to continue living. But when the person on the bridge has asked that we not talk to them about God, out of respect to their wishes, we need to stop the God talk.

In the conversation that followed the simulation, the helper was initially adamant that she had a mandate to share the gospel. As gently as possible, I explained that I understood her desire, but she didn't have a mandate to kill people with the gospel. What if instead of hammering the person at risk with a faith agenda, we meet them instead, where they are. Isn't that what Jesus did? The woman at the well and Zacchaeus in a sycamore tree are just two of many examples of how he engaged people in their journey, and their lives were transformed. What if instead of losing the person because of our agenda, we had found a way to help him avoid a tragedy. We want to validate the pain without humiliating them for a lack of faith (at least from our point of view)? How might the conversation a couple of days later have gone when the helper called to check on the person.

Helper: Hi this is _____. I am just calling to see how you are doing.

PAR: I'm much better now. I did see my doctor as you suggested, and my wife and I had a long talk. I don't know that we can save the marriage, but we are both willing to try.

Helper: I am so glad to hear that. Did you have an opportunity to talk with HR about moving to that less stressful department?

PAR: That might take some time, but I am taking two weeks off and using part of my vacation time to go on that weekend men's retreat with the group your brother is in. I talked with him last night. He's a nice guy.

Helper: Yes, he is a good big brother to me too.

PAR: Can I ask you something?

Helper: Sure…

PAR: Why did you stop?

Helper: What do you mean?

PAR: When I was on that bridge, why did you stop?

Helper: I stopped because I was concerned for your safety.

PAR: But why? One hundred other cars went by and they didn't stop. Why would you be concerned for my safety when no one else was? You didn't even know me…

Helper: It doesn't matter that I didn't know you. I knew I didn't want you to die.

PAR: But why?

Helper: Well to be honest, I believe that God has a purpose for your life.

PAR: I sure wish I knew what that purpose is....

Helper: You can.

PAR: How?

If this were a book on evangelism we would call such conversation an open-door invitation. My point is this, the *Listen Learn Lead* model is about meeting people where they are. It's not a quick fix for all the pain, and a successful intervention doesn't mean that all the problems miraculously disappear. L3 is a first aid lifesaving model, just as CPR is. After the immediate risk to life is addressed, there will many times still be a need for ongoing work with a therapist or pastoral care counselor. Follow up may also include a visit to the doctor. These are roles that someone else will play; the helper does not carry the weight alone. The intervention is simply the first step in moving the person at risk in the right direction. Hopefully, knowing this, you as a potential helper can take a deep breath of relief in knowing that you don't have to solve all the problems.

As previously mentioned in chapter two, during my conversation with the person on the airplane, I asked the man if he was a person of faith. Sometimes I will ask, "Do you have a faith background?" The reason I ask is not for the purpose of converting them to my faith if they say no, but so that I have a better understanding of what their potential support resources might be that they are already familiar with. If they say yes, I might ask, "How has your faith helped you when you experienced challenges in the past?" or "What is a favorite verse of scripture that has helped you when things were difficult?" But again, I am always careful. The person may say yes to the faith question but have great anger toward God. In the moment of crisis, I am not there to provide apologetics or in any way attempt to defend or prove the truth of religious doctrines such as "God is good" or "why bad things happen to good people". When the risk is imminent those are conversations better left to another place and time.

Mark 8:18 reads, "Do you have eyes but fail to see, and ears but fail to hear?" There have been times when I have been engaged in beautiful discussions of faith and questions of theology after the immediate risk of suicide has subsided. Often such questions have been raised by the person that was hurting.

I suppose it is because of the work I do that I often have individuals that will start a conversation with, "I have a friend…" The truth is they are looking for answers for themselves and they covertly want me to help them without my being aware that I am doing so. In those times I am reminded of Mark 8:18. Though I am more than willing, they are not sure. Suicide is the elephant in the room; they want to talk about difficult things, but they also need to know they are safe to do so with me. As the helper, we must present ourselves with the attitude that we are open to such discussions. I am always careful not to blurt out the question of suicide. I do want to pace them as best I can. But as the conversation continues, I will eventually ask the question, "So, is this a friend that we are talking about or is this you?"

Like the elephant in the room, I can't help but think about the humans that no one or very few are willing to see; they're all around us. The truth is we may see the pain; we may know that something is wrong. Many times, we may even offer care or show our concern and yet still fail to ask one central question that has the power to transform a hurting individual's mental, emotional, and even spiritual state of mind. When we truly understand the power of the question, we will find the courage to ask, "Are you having thoughts of suicide?"

Just this afternoon I received a phone call from a friend who has a friend that had recently lost his wife and was himself experiencing financial and health issues. My friend stated this man was "not acting like himself and seemed rather distant." He was concerned the man may be suicidal. He asked, "What should I do?" My bottom line response, ask the man if he was having thoughts of suicide and then listen. Of course, professional follow up care may be required, but the first step is to ask the question.

As previously stated, 1 in 20 people have suicidal thoughts each year. Thankfully, most do not act upon those thoughts, however, the risk is increased with mild to moderate depression and other life changing circumstances such as the loss of a family member, financial or health related issues. While the suicide rate among America's troops and veterans is regularly reported, suicidal ideation is not the exclusive domain of those who serve our country. For example, a Danish study revealed the "risk of suicide doubles for women suffering from infertility". Imagine for a moment how the anguish is unintentionally exacerbated with friends and family engaged in baby-talk at a shower for a newborn, a discussion that for all others brings great joy. Think about the pain of a teenager who is bullied at school and appears to have no close friends. According to the CDC and studies from Yale University "bully victims are up to nine times more likely to die from suicide". I will not inundate you with stats on various risk factors, the point is made. Hurting people are all around us; we can clearly see this. The elephant in the room is the reality that few are willing to broach the subject of suicide.

I know many individuals and organizations are focused on the reduction of stigma and, yet stigma remains an issue. Thus, over the past few years I have made the deliberate choice not to focus my time and energy on fighting stigma; I leave that to others. Rather I have chosen to focus on the reality of the human condition. In working with more than 24,000 soldiers and training 10,000 mental health professionals and others in the civilian community, I have constantly driven home the reality that suicide is part of the human condition just as any pain is. Denying the reality of our condition does not change the reality. By honestly addressing the issues in a safe environment, I never have to address stigma; it simply fades away.

Two individuals were whispering back and forth during a workshop. Finally, I had enough; "Is there something you would like to say for the benefit of all of us?" The young lady spoke up, "What you said was wrong?" I responded, "Oh, I'm sorry. What was that?" "You said, 'How does that make you feel?' What you should have said is, 'How do you feel about that?'" At this point I knew where she was headed and asked her, "Please, enlighten us." The lady went on to explain that the first question implies that the person is not in control of how they feel and the "right way" empowers them, that they are in control. I certainly understand her point of view. However, the reality is that the person at risk doesn't feel empowered, they feel like they should die. We, as helpers, must be comfortable being there with them in that dark place and be careful of patronizing words. But at the same time, if we are overly concerned with semantics, we may not say anything. Several survivors after a loss have shared in tears, "I was afraid to say anything." When we are demonstrating appropriate care, I am certain the person at risk is not analyzing every nuance of the words we say the way a clinician does in the classroom.

Many of the interventions I have done have come by referral from individuals that were not sure what to say. But they didn't let that stop them from doing something. They called someone that would know what to say and do. Often stigma will keep a potential helper from speaking up. While we do need to work at addressing stigma, we should not let stigma stop us from doing something such as calling people that can help. There is no shame or disgrace in asking others to help you help someone. This too is part of the human condition. We all need help, even helpers.

One of our greatest challenges has been engaging the faith community to join us in the mission of saving human lives. Some have done so, and we have seen incredible and very positive outcomes, oftentimes within days of hosting a workshop. But we need many more to come along side as battle buddies to host the Intervene Challenge and the *Listen Learn Lead* workshops.

Recently, in my hometown we began a new campaign called ONE in 100. The goal is that over the next several years we will train 1,100 of the 110,000 members of our community. I can't help but believe that there is a tipping point that will be the catalyst for substantially reducing and even eradicating suicide. I just don't know what that tipping point is, but we will when we get there.

Speaking of tipping points and knowing when we get there, I am reminded of a verse from chapter 11 of Hebrews, the faith chapter.

> *"By faith Abraham, when called to go to a place he would later receive as his inheritance, obeyed, and went, even though he did not know where he was going."*

Often, it seems I don't know where I am going in trying to reduce suicide in my community or even in attempting to help those that are filled with hopelessness. But I also believe that because I have prepared myself for the task (2 Timothy 2:16), I can step out in faith and I will have the words that are appropriate for the moment (Luke 12:12). When we get to the place we need to go, both I and the person I am helping will know it. It's the place of life, hope, and a future.

In the last section of this chapter I wish to address a matter that seems most intervention models are hesitant to address. Pornography is killing people. Unfortunately, when the evils of porn are addressed the point is missed entirely. A January 2018 article in the New York Post was entitled *Why Porn Stars Are Dying at An Alarming Rate*. In the last half of 2017 five porn stars died by suicide. According to the article, "the young women struggled with a lack of steady work. There are now more porn actors than ever, thanks to increasing platforms, as well as growing mainstream acceptance. That makes the competition fierce." Sadly, I must say that it is not the competition that is killing these young women and it is not just the actors that take their lives. The consumers do too.

Dr. Ted Roberts is a pastor and former U.S. Marine Corps Fighter Pilot. From the violent jungles of the Vietnam war to the hand to hand combat of getting free from sexual bondage, Dr. Roberts knows what it takes to conquer hell at close range. In his Conquer Series for men he shares about the mechanics of the mind regarding sexual addiction. These same principles are applicable in the work of suicide intervention. In fact, the two are intimately related. Dr. Roberts shares, "What fires together wires together." Many men that I have worked with have sought to ease their pain through porn resulting in only further escalation of their pain. From my personal experience I too know the vicious cycle of momentary pleasure followed by overwhelming pain. The dark pit of despair and hopelessness that comes with porn, has led many men to suicide. Knowing this reality brings new meaning to the words of Deuteronomy 30:19. "I have set before you life and death, blessing and cursing; therefore, choose life, that both you and your descendants may live." The firing and wiring that men allow to take place in their mind is passed down in their DNA to their children. The good news is that individuals, both men and women, that struggle with addiction can be renewed in their minds. It takes time and effort, but it is possible.

When we run on emotion the limbic system of the brain is controlling our minds. However, the limbic system is not capable of making rational decisions. The outcome when it is in control is rarely good. Road rage, poor buying decisions, affairs, shooting up a church, outburst at the spouse or kids, dysfunctional families - all related to the hijacking of the prefrontal lobes by the limbic part of the brain; it's like a mutiny on a Navy ship. The same thing happens with thoughts of suicide. The executive decision-making part of the brain has been hijacked. Research over the past 20 years on the

Neuroplasticity of the brain is affirming what the scripture has shown us for 2000 years. Because of lack of control over the limbic generated emotions the "conscience has been seared as with a hot iron". But there is hope we can be renewed in the spirit of our mind. Finding victory doesn't happen by accident, but by understanding the weapons of our warfare.

Suicide is a legacy that leaves broken hearts asking questions that often cannot be answered. The faith community has the opportunity and responsibility of providing broken people with the resources that can help them in their battle. For this reason, my work in suicide intervention has led to the establishment of weekend retreats for men that we call Warrior Chapel. To learn more visit WarriorChapel.org. Through Warrior Chapel we seek to lead men to the understanding that they can live victorious lives Through a three-day weekend retreat format, we gather with other men that are ready to win the greatest battle of all - the one in our own hearts and minds. Using Dr. Roberts Conquer Series as our primary curriculum, we address one of the primary reasons men today often feel like prisoners of war. We address the battle in our minds that has left chaos in our spirit and collateral damage in our relationships that for some has led to thoughts of suicide.

2 Samuel 23 gives a list of names that have been remembered for 3,000 years; there were 37 in all. They were known as David's Mighty Warriors. Often weary

from battle, they continued to stand and fight when others ran. Matthew reminds us of violent men who take the kingdom by force and Paul tells us in Romans not to let sin reign in our mortal bodies. Warriors that win battles, subject themselves to rigorous training. They know the ways of the enemy and are disciplined in the skills to defend and advance the mission to which they are called. In our day, that which is most needed are men who are willing to violently attack the reign of sin in our own minds; men who are willing to fight for a legacy worth remembering. True Victory is a choice that is made only by concerted effort in the battle. Are you one who is prepared to win?

KENNETH KOON

Disaster and the
Increased Risk of Suicide

Ready are you? What know you of ready?
Yoda

Suicidologists have studied the effects of disaster related suicide since London was blitzed with bombs in World War II. For a period after the 57 days of nightly bombing, suicide and even drunkenness greatly decreased. Similar findings were revealed after 9-11, Hurricanes Ike and Katrina. In the years ahead, we will likely find similar results with tragedies like the Los Vegas shooting in 2017 that left 57 dead or the Parkland, Florida school shooting on Valentine's Day 2018.

Manmade chaos can often be more traumatizing to individuals and communities than natural disaster because the human element is involved. With storms there is the weather channel to alert us to incoming danger. Often such is not the case with human instigated acts of terror. Two weeks after the Parkland, Florida shooting I was speaking to a group of Soldiers in Richmond, Virginia; I mentioned the Parkland tragedy. After I spoke, a Soldier came to me with tears in her eyes. She lived near Parkland and her daughter had friends that were involved in the events that happened that day. Sadly, for the people of Parkland, Valentine's Day will forever be a memorial day. For some remembering February 14 as anything other than a memorial will be a tremendous challenge. For others it is my prayer that Valentine's Day will be transformed into an even higher meaning as a day when we remember that love conquerors evil.

There is always a brief time after disaster that people pull together. We often see this in microcosm when a family member dies. Differences are set aside; there is a coming together for the common good, but then weeks later after probate, the WILL is read, and all hell breaks loose, words fly, and fragile relationships are shattered beyond repair. In the same way there is a honeymoon or pulling together phenomenon that takes place with disaster, but at some point, the honeymoon is over. In this regard, it is like the soldier that earns a purple heart saving his battle buddy, but years later takes his own life.

In 1999, due to faulty data, The New England Journal of Medicine retracted their statement that suicide rates increase after natural disaster. They were correct, suicide does increase. But because of a retraction, others naturally assumed that disaster does not increase the risk of suicide. However, a bit of common sense is in order here. Take large scale disaster out of the equation for a moment. We know that risk of suicide increases whenever there is an unfavorable change in circumstances, particularly major losses, like the loss of a family member, loss of a home, loss of a job and so forth. This being the case, why would we think suicide does not increase when natural disaster causes such losses?

More recent research (2012) from the Australian Institute for Suicide Research and Prevention concluded that "the effects of natural disasters include stress and somatic and mental health problems, including suicidal ideation." An August 2015 report Suicide After Disaster by the Substance Abuse Mental Health Services Administration (SAMHSA) revealed a reduction in suicidal risk factors stating, "this effect might not be long-lasting." They go on to state, "This may be explained by the elevated level of social support and care available in this period." When the care and support go away, as it always does, the loss is not forgotten, and the consequences of loss remain even if the city is rebuilt to a better state than before. We can rebuild cities with enough money and manpower, rebuilding lives takes a more powerful resource.

While the statisticians crunch the numbers, I refuse to sit idly by, hoping that suicide will not increase after disaster. Again, common sense and a compassionate heart should prevail. Hurricane Harvey resulted in half a million people seeking assistance from FEMA for repairs to their homes, 30,000 that needed temporary housing, and many of those who did not lose their cars in floods lost them for inability to pay the car note because they are out of a job at the mom and pop restaurant that couldn't recover. Additionally, families were robbed at gun point by those they thought were coming to save them, post-traumatic stress increased, and at least 60 families buried their dead that were killed by the storm. Any statistician that would argue that natural disaster does not increase suicide has their head in the sand. Just months after Harvey, we are working in partnership with the Stronger Alliance to take the *Listen Learn Lead* workshop to Houston in a preemptive measure to address the suicidal ideation that is sure to come. Churches that send out Disaster Relief Teams would do well to also train their teams in suicide intervention. The skills they learn will be used in those communities that have been devastated by disaster.

Find a Reason to Live

Perseverance, Secret of All Triumphs
Victor Hugo

When a new show came out on Netflix called *13 Reasons Why*, it set off a firestorm of discussion within the school and mental health community. I personally had no desire to watch the show, though one colleague highly recommended that I should because of the work I do. Some parents shared that they did watch the series with their children, and a healthy discussion followed. My concern was not that it would cause healthy teens to suddenly want to take their lives, but rather that a middle schooler might watch alone that was already having thoughts of suicide.

From what I have gathered, another season is planned; hopefully, it will offer healthy solutions; the first season did not. The show simply did what every suicide does - it passed the pain on to someone else and seemed to express that suicide was the only option. The truth is, suicide is not an option - it's an end. Ends are not options. Think about it, when has any other option been so final as suicide. You can always choose a new career if your first option doesn't work out. Heck, every other option in life always opens the doors to other options. Not so with suicide. Therefore, suicide is not the solution because it's not an option. It's an end. The story is over (at least for the person that takes their life).

Through my own battle and working with others on the battlefield of personal pain, I have concluded that suicide is not about wanting to die. How ironic is that? Suicide is not about wanting to die, but it is all about not knowing how to live amid physical, emotional, or mental pain or the hurt of broken or lost relationships. Everyone that I have ever worked with that attempted suicide said that they regret that they ever tried. The reality is you can choose life. You don't have to cave because of the bullies or what others do to you. You can find the strength to overcome. You can choose life instead of death. But you must find your reason. A person may have 13 reasons why they want to do die, but one good reason can overcome the 13 bad ones.

The show, *13 Reasons Why* perpetuates a fallacy, a myth that through suicide I will have a greater voice than I could ever have in life. The sad reality is suicide takes away your voice. And as most parents who have lost children will tell you – my son's/daughter's name is rarely mentioned simply because others don't know what to do and how to respond. Teenagers that have this idea that suicide will give them a voice fail to understand that it won't. They simply become a number out of the 44,000 others that do the same every year.

I often share with teens that are struggling, you really want to make a difference - then continue to live. Continue to press on when the voices say give up. Develop strong lungs that you will need to be a mighty voice speaking up for those who are hurting, for those who are bullied, for those with mental health challenges, for anyone on the edge of the abyss. You find in your life one powerful reason to live, and it will overcome 13 reasons why you would ever consider suicide.

My 8th and 9th grade years of high school were awkward. I was teased for wearing headgear to correct a severe overbite, Butch and Eddie would steal my lunch money, and others wanted to pick fights. Then Randy, the captain of the football team, took me under his wings, and after that no one bothered me. I started lifting weights, and by the time I was a senior, I and a couple of my friends were the ones protecting the kids that were bullied. It certainly helped that I had set a few high school powerlifting records. In all honesty, having a friend that cared helped me move in the right direction, but I had to choose to make a positive healthy decision that I was going to change my life for the better. I had to decide that others were not going to defeat me. Unfortunately, some choose to make poor decisions whether it be suicide or a school shooting rampage. Thomas Edison said, "Many of life's failures are people who did not realize how close they were to success when they gave up." If we are going to find a reason to live, no matter how long it takes, we must first choose to never give up.

CAREGIVER RESILIENCE

When the well's dry, we know the worth of water.
Benjamin Franklin

He may wear an S on his chest and leap tall buildings at a single bound, but even Superman had a weakness. Kryptonite, the radioactive rock of his home planet, would bring Superman to his knees every time. Kryptonite for the caregiver is not a rock, but a mindset, wherein we think that we are Superman or Superwoman. With such mindset we view taking care of the needs of others as more important than taking care of our own. We go and go till there is nothing left in the tank, and we find ourselves stranded on the highway of great expectations.

I never recall Superman ever asking for help or refusing to rip off his tie and glasses when duty called. Perhaps Clark Kent developed his Superman mindset early on from too many episodes of *Underdog*, "Here I come to save the day!" Looking back, I realize that for years I have had that same mindset. I raised my four boys on the family motto that "We are the Can-Do-Koons. We are on a quest to be our best."

I have never liked asking for help, but I have learned over the past five years that I must be willing to receive the help of others. Doing so helps to maintain my own health so that I can continue to help others. It's not an easy reality for me to accept. Just last night I had to finally blow off steam to a friend, and I then apologized for "dumping" on him. He responded by saying, "Well first... I didn't hear any dumping!! We all need someone to talk to and vent; as the suicide prevention trainer you know this. So, as a friend, battle buddy and one who has been there, please feel free to vent as needed."

Sherry too, has always had that Superwoman mindset and found it hard to ask for help. One of my greatest regrets as a husband is my own failure to recognize those times when she was asking, but I didn't have ears to hear. She has carried a heavy load because of the work I do. There have been many times in the middle of the night when she couldn't sleep because I had been called to aid someone in crisis with a gun. In many ways I see how she has suffered from secondary traumatic stress that was induced vicariously through me. I have seen the same in the wives of MPs immediately following the Dallas and New Orleans tragedies in the summer of 2016. Several spouses told their husbands they had to choose – them or their career because they couldn't take it anymore.

I am thankful that, like me, Sherry has a few good friends that allow her space to vent. Such friends are a rare blessing. They do far more than they realize by simply being present in our lives. Through such friends we find encouragement and renewed strength to press on. They don't try to change the subject when they find out what I do. I learned early on that with many people I can't talk about what I do. I even had an individual that was so full of superstition that he would not give to the cause because he was afraid it might open the door to a spirit of suicide in his family. I hope that individual is getting counseling somewhere.

The essential point is this. I am thankful for a few good folks who allow me to just be a Clark Kent, no cape, no S on my chest, just Clark Kent. They may be few, but a few is enough. The reality is that Superman does not exists. What makes an individual soar to great heights is not superpowers and a cape but the ability to surround oneself with other ordinary human beings that realize that we are better together and that the whole is greater than the sum of the parts.

The study of resilience has always been fascinating to me. How is it that some people, like Army Sergeant, Kortney Clemons can lose a leg in Iraq and go on to become a US Paralympian, while others come back from war with no visible wounds but end up taking their lives? One thing I have learned in my work is that all wounds are not visible, but they are physical. Trauma physically rewires the brain.

Even the mental health professionals will admit to an incomplete understanding of why some people are more resilient than others. Meg Jay, PhD writes in

SuperNormal, The Untold Story of Adversity and Resilience, "Resilience is most certainly a phenomenon: a highly individual experience that we will never be able to reduce to a formula or an algorithm."[xv] Jay describes the *supernormals* as those that have "daily struggles above and beyond what we think of as average and expectable, but their subsequent successes exceed expectations too. They beat the odds, they live improbable lives, and after decades of academic study no one knows quite how."

While the study of resilience fascinates me, I confess as a Chaplain that I am a novice academically at understanding how the amygdala processes emotions or the thalamus relays motor and sensory signals to the cerebral cortex. I tend to think in word pictures and much more elementary terms. A man wanted to argue with me that his dad's generation (a WWII veteran) was much tougher than the generation of soldiers today saying, "None of my dad's buddies took their lives after the war. They didn't have PTSD. These guys today – well it's just in their head!" I responded with, "Sir, you are mistaken. Many of your dad's generation have killed themselves, and they did have PTSD. They just didn't talk about it." PTSD has been a reality in every war, we just called it by other names, such as shell shock or nostalgia. And yes, soldiers have taken their own lives during or after every war. News clippings from the mid-1800s are replete with accounts of suicide during and after the Civil War. One such account is that of Philip St. George Cocke, the wealthiest Virginia land owner and a brigadier general. After a demotion to Colonel, he took his life. While it has been widely reported that more than 100,000 Vietnam Veterans have died by suicide, we do know with certainty from a CDC study that at least 3,752 have died by suicide as of 1996. The number over the past 21 years is not yet conclusive but is no doubt much higher.

The brain is composed of 100 billion neurons with 10,000 synaptic bridges connecting each neuron. According to my math, that's one million-billion whatever that number is; that's a lot of bridges. When the wiring gets frayed through trauma, good luck putting the parts in order. I asked the argumentative man, "Is that your new Ford Mustang? Let's pop the hood and move some wires around. What do you think would happen?" He responded, "It wouldn't work right, and I would be upset." "But why? It's just in your hood."

Stating the problem is just in your head is like telling someone having a heart attack, the problem is just in your chest. If we say people that are depressed just need to think positive thoughts, why don't we do the same when grandmother falls and breaks her hip? "Come on grandma; just walk it off." Daniel Amen, MD is a clinical neuroscientist, psychiatrist, and brain imaging expert who heads the world-renowned Amen Clinics. In one of his studies he found left temporal lobe abnormalities in 62% of his patients who had serious suicidal thoughts or actions.[xvi]

What do these stats have to do with a section on caregiver resilience? First, compassionate caregivers understand that there is more to mental health than simply trying to have positive thoughts, the *it's all in your head* mentality isn't helpful when negative neural pathways in the brain have been created by depression, pain, or trauma. I also share stats in hopes that you will keep learning. I am always inspired by the number of soldiers, First Responders and homemakers that return to school later in life to earn advanced degrees in the helping professions. Many of them do so because of their personnel experiences with trauma. They have taken the pain in their own lives and discovered a passion and purpose to help others. One friend recently completed training with Eastern Mennonite University called Strategies for Trauma Awareness and Resilience (STAR). STAR aims to strengthen the capacity of individuals, organizations, and communities to understand the impacts of trauma, and build resilience at the personal, community and societal levels. I hope to participate in STAR soon. Currently, I am working through a series of courses with The National Institute for the Clinical Application of Behavioral Medicine. NICABM offers learning opportunities in online video presentations on a wide range of topic matters. The point being - *Never stop learning!* This ongoing pursuit of knowledge has worked to restore resilience in my personal life while equipping me to better help others in the journey.

Counselors, Chaplains, law enforcement, EMS, 911 operators and all others that work with those in crisis know there is a cost to caring. Individuals suffering from compassion fatigue can exhibit the same signs and symptoms as the individuals they seek to help. Daily helping people when they are at the worst point in life puts a tremendous toll on the helper's mental and emotional reserves. Therefore, it is imperative that helpers find meaningful ways to strengthen themselves. There is a plethora of books on resilience and care for the caregiver. So, I will simply share a few things that I have found to be most helpful to me.

As I have previously shared, my son encouraged me to get back in the gym. Working out has been a lifelong passion, but when I hit the wall mentally and emotionally, I stopped doing the very thing that I had loved all my life. Exercise produces naturally occurring "feel good" hormones and helps clear the mind of clutter. When I returned to the gym a few days later, I penned in my journal, "Under the cold iron of the local gym, the embers of life were stoked once again into flame."

Equine therapy has been a great resilience restorer for both me and my wife, Sherry. I am indebted to Jeanne Bowers and Cyndi Gall and the horses for working with us to help me stay balanced. Working with the horses and trained counselors is a great program for individuals with PTSD as well as other mental and physical challenges. Some of the exercises have also had direct application on strengthening the marriage relationship. I work from a home office, but it is Sherry's home too. Through one of the equine exercises I came to realize how important it was for me to get out of the house sometimes for Sherry's sake. I know she loves me deeply, but there are times when she needs a break from taking care of others, myself included.

My equine friend, Jeanne, is also one of the handful of people that call to check on me when I send out the "Bat Signal". Instead of making an appointment to debrief with one therapist, I will put a picture of the old Batman signal in the sky on my social media account. Some people will hit the like button, others will make a comment, but a few like Jeanne know that it is the signal to call so that I can unpack mentally after a challenging intervention. There have been times when three or four would call. By the time the last does, my head is clear, I thank them for the call and we laugh that they didn't win first place, maybe next time. However, you choose to do it, make sure that you have within your circle three or four people that you can unpack with on a regular basis. The work of caring for others is a work we cannot do alone.

For several years I have lived by a personal mantra – Don't waste kilowatts. I came to accept the fact that I only have so much energy to offer others; I must reserve energy to take care of my own needs too. I shared this with a family member that was caring for her husband that had advanced Alzheimer's. It was evident that she had reached the limit of what she could handle on her own. The family encouraged her to place her husband in a fulltime care facility. She continues to visit her husband daily, but she is now stronger because of her decision to take care of herself too. Selfcare is not a selfish act.

The American theologian, Reinhold Niebuhr, had a prayer that he offered throughout his career. This prayer was later picked up by various support groups, such as Alcoholics Anonymous; it is known today as the Serenity Prayer.

God, grant me the serenity to accept the things I cannot change, Courage to change the things I can, And wisdom to know the difference.

Finally, the foundation upon which all other personal resilience in my life has been built is the belief that there is a God and that God is good. Numerous university studies and medical research demonstrates the power of faith in strengthening the mind and body. Captain Nathan Self is a former US Army Ranger and a highly decorated soldier for his actions in the battle of Takur Ghar, Afghanistan. He had survived combat, and he had come home, but he soon had thoughts of how he would kill himself. But ask him today what saved him, and he will tell you: faith in God.

I WILL INTERVENE

I Will Listen, I Will Learn, I Will Lead...I WILL INTERVENE! After a workshop at Ft. Dix, New Jersey, a solitary soldier stood in the back of the room and shouted these words. Then the soldier next to him did the same, and the one next to him. By the time it got to the front row fifty soldiers had stood and done the same. With the last one they shouted in one mighty voice, I WILL INTEREVENE. The Intervene Challenge has since become the mantra that participants say together at the conclusion of the L3 workshops. It is also the banner under which we now provide all our workshops.

Through this book and the *Listen Learn Lead* Intervention Training Workshops, I have sought to turn on the light of awareness where it can best make a difference. Nearly 200 times a year I find myself in a one-on-one, using the model with a person at immediate risk of self-harm. On a few occasions I have found myself in an intervention with workshop attendees during a lunch break or after the class. My passion is working with people. What drains me is not people, but the broken systems within which I find hurting people. I often feel like a medic on the battlefield trying to help the wounded while avoiding being shot by friendly fire. While I am not the one to change the system, perhaps you are. You may be the one that can convince communities that saving lives is an important matter worthy of their time and giving dollars. Perhaps it is my military mindset or the fact that I don't like politics when it is killing people, so I struggle in this regard. A pastor asked what our cost is for bringing the Challenge to his church. I told him, "That depends on whether we do it now or later." He responded, "So you offer a discount if we book now?" "No Sir. We charge the same amount regardless of when we do the workshop, but if someone dies because you waited, that would be a costly workshop." That's not a strongarm sales pitch; it is simply the truth that we have experienced firsthand. I look back over more than 800 suicide interventions, and I like to think that perhaps we have made a difference, but there is so much more that needs to be done and more people and resources are needed if we hope to sustain an ongoing reduction in suicide.

On the battlefield there are various branches and within the branches there are specialized units each with a specific function. You may be the one that can help plant the seed within our government, within the schools, the churches, the corporate and civic community. I pray that someone is listening; it will take an army to stem the tide. On my part, I will simply keep working one-on-one with those that are hurting and teaching others to do the same. Perhaps in time a champion will emerge that can change the culture of health on a grander scale to fill communities across the land with people that are willing to intervene.

Several years ago, in my hometown, there was an incident involving the accidental incineration of radioactive material in a crematory. Immediately, EPA personnel from Atlanta were on site in their white MOP suits with their Geiger counters. They quarantined the building and sent employees to the hospital for observation. They were prepared for the crisis moment. When it comes to suicide crisis, most people are not prepared. Every year for three years I would knock on the door of a church urging them to host a workshop for their members. I shared that it could also be an outreach to the community. I was told the church was focusing on mission work in China. In any case, they were not willing to allocate time or funding to such a program. It was only after the loss of a youth in the church that they committed to doing a workshop a few weeks later. They finally realized the importance of preparation. Sadly, life teaches us in many ways that listening too late is too costly; this is always the case with a suicide that could have been averted.

We call our workshops a Challenge for several reasons. As of December 2017, more than 10,000 individuals across the country have participated in various workshops we have taught throughout the US, but it has been a challenge attracting that number of people to workshops on a subject that few people want to talk about. It is also a challenge for many people that attend. While the workshop is not a therapy session, there are always tears from some participants, the ones that have experienced loss. Many also begin to see ways that they might have stopped the tragedy from happening, and this is painful too.

Then there is the challenge of rallying corporations, churches, civic groups, and individuals to provide financial support so that we can train even more people. Suicide intervention training is unfortunately not a high priority until it is too late. Recently I challenged my hometown community with a question, "What is the will of our community when it comes to the unnecessary loss of life?" I'm not talking about a few passionate individuals that support the work or folks like Kevin Briggs, Kevin Hines, or myself, but what about the community as a whole? How do you determine the collective will of a community? There is only one way. It is through the financial support communities show for the things that it says are important. It's more than just "ataboys" and thousands of likes on Facebook. It's more than simply saying I appreciate what you do, and I am glad you are the one doing it. I wish this were not the case, but a non-profit like any business model cannot exist on Facebook likes alone.

Turning the tide on suicide will take the effort of many people working as one. No one person or organization can stop this epidemic. The Intervene Challenge seeks to rally an army of passionate individuals that are ready willing and able to make a difference. Some will be financial supporters that have the gift of giving. Others are organizers that can bring community together to address the issues in hometowns across America, and others are the courageous individuals that simply want to learn the skills for the sake of their family and friends. Through the Intervene Challenge we are training people to save people.

Listen Learn Lead is just one of serval curriculums that we offer in the Challenge. I was initiated into the intervention training world as a facilitator of Applied Suicide Intervention Skills Training (ASIST). The Army sent me to ASIST Trainer training shortly after returning to service at the age of 45. ASIST is a premier two-day workshop with more than one million people trained worldwide. As a Master ASIST Trainer, I love the ASIST curriculum and teach it as often as possible. ASIST does require two consecutive days and no less than 45 days of community prep time but is well worth the effort. Learn more at ASISTworkshop.com.

We also offer several 2-hour workshops and 30-minute briefings that serve as introductions and preparation for moving a community or organization to the next level with our one or two-day workshops.

Mental Health First Aid (MHFA) is an excellent one-day workshop that we have taught in Law Enforcement and church settings. Mental Health First Aid helps participants assist someone experiencing a mental health or substance use-related crisis. In the Mental Health First Aid course, participants learn risk factors and warning signs for mental health and addiction concerns, strategies for how to help someone in both crisis and non-crisis situations and where to turn for help.

Finally, we offer the Listen Learn Lead curriculum. Clients served have included churches, schools, civic groups, hospitals, military units, law enforcement, fire, and EMS agencies. The standardized workshop is intended to be taught in a five-hour block. Typically, we will start the morning at 9 a.m. and conclude around 4:00 in the afternoon. Due to the content we limit participation to those 16 years and older and register no more than 50 participants in each workshop. I have taught the workshop since inception, however, beginning in 2018, we are offering a Train the Trainer program that will hopefully expand our outreach to equip an even larger network of care givers nationwide.

Individuals that have taken our workshops are now making a difference in communities across the US. They have discovered, like I did, that the courage to ask is the power to save. Applying the principles of listening, learning, and leading saves lives. But these same principles have been applied in other relationships with great success as well, to build stronger marriages, reduce toxic leadership within corporations and strengthen parent child relationships. Listen Learn Lead is a model with great potential to transform families, corporations, and entire communities. My hope is that you will take the next step in joining us for the live workshop. Better yet, organize a workshop and let's work together to transform your community.

Listen Learn Lead Workshop

Listen-Learn-Lead© (L3) Suicide Intervention is a one-day workshop in suicide intervention. L3 will benefit individuals from all walks of life and offers applications in various life situations. Armed Forces Mission and Stop Suicide USA are the exclusive providers of L3 Training, facilitated by L3 certified instructors.

SYNOPSIS

Intervention begins with listening. Leading the person at risk to safety is the desired outcome. Leading is embedded in listening and learning. Asking the suicide question opens the door to further learning as the helper continues to listen. The person at risk is also learning. They are learning that they are not alone, that someone cares and that there is hope.

PRIMARY ENABLING OBJECTIVE

Participants will gain the skills and confidence to save individuals at risk of suicide.

First Hour

- Increase personal awareness of the community impact of suicide
- Understand the importance of developing a culture of community health
- Gain insight into the questions asked in each phase of the L^3 model

Second Hour

- Recognize the steps to transitioning through the L^3 model
- Understand the importance of building rapport that enables a successful intervention
- Practice the model through roleplay and simulation exercises

Third Hour

- Discuss fears that impede willingness to intervene
- Evaluate the myths that impact societal and helper responses to suicide
- Examine cultural differences that challenge ability to intervene

Fourth Hour

- Apply learning to better understand potential risk
- Learn how the brain responds to Post Traumatic Stress increasing risk of suicide
- Attempt to complete a brain response exercise given a PTS condition

Fifth Hour

- Demonstrate skills to intervene through roleplay and simulation exercise
- Identify the steps in transitioning to safety
- Summarize the various community resources for further assistance as needed

Important reminder

L3 is intended to provide general information for educational purposes only. The L3 presentation is not a substitute for medical or other professional care, and you should not use the information in place of a visit, call consultation or the advice of your physician or other healthcare provider. The L3 presentation is not intended to create or establish ministerial duty for law enforcement, EMS, teachers, counselors, or other individuals who must implement a given policy in accordance with their employer or the law.

To learn more visit ListenLearnLead.org

IN MEMORY

Recently, I was in a car dealership shopping for a Rapid Response Vehicle for Armed Forces Mission. A man I did not know called my name. The first words he spoke, "You did Kyle's funeral." I responded, "Yes, I did. He died January 13, 2016, a Wednesday afternoon." "Wow, that was two years ago, and you remember the day." "I can't forget."

I don't remember the specific dates of the successful interventions, but I have plenty of dates in my head of those I have lost because I did not know they were hurting. I share now the words that I spoke at Kyle's memorial in the hopes that others might find comfort in their own loss.

Today is a very difficult day for everyone in this room. It really is beyond words to describe. We come here today with many emotions - many conflicting emotions. Hope and hopelessness - fond memories and overwhelming grief - questions without answers. Perhaps even anger. Anger with ourselves, anger with Kyle, and no doubt, there are some here today who are angry with God. All the above is normal and to be expected in times like today. As I often tell Soldiers, "These are the normal responses to abnormal circumstances."

This is not the way it was supposed to be…the way we hoped it would be. Kyle should be with us today. He should be by Lauren's side in May when his precious little girl is born and on his birthday May 3rd. He should be with us on the holidays and the vacations. He should be going to work tomorrow. Today goes beyond our ability to fully comprehend.

Kyle had an infectious laughter that made others laugh and an incredible sense of humor. He had a certain way of smiling at those he loved. As Cheryl said, "He was a sweet, loving son who had a strong desire to better himself." Kyle Lovett wanted to do what was right, but he never took credit for the good things he did. He never felt worthy, and he never wanted to disappoint others.

I never had the honor of knowing Kyle, yet over the past few days I have had the opportunity to learn who he was. Hearing the stories and learning about his experiences helps give me a picture of the man, Joshua Kyle Lovett, but it also helps me catch just a glimpse of possibly some of the reasons we are here today.

When Kyle deployed, his journey into darkness began. As Barry said, "He came back a man, but a different person." He wasn't the same. War has a way of doing that to a person. It was also along that time that he lost his brother, Dustin, and somehow Kyle took on a responsibility for Dustin's death that was not his to take. The cumulative effect of traumatic stress wore at his heart and mind for several years up until a few days ago. Some of the times when he was most like the old Kyle were when he had Brody, his service dog, by his side. In those times Kyle was like a kid again smiling, laughing, and loving life. Yet the pain was always there.

It has been said that "suffering reveals what is in our hearts and takes the one who suffers to the edge of eternity". I have worked with 25,000 soldiers over the past 5 years and have conducted hundreds of suicide interventions. In that time, I have come to believe that suffering has a way of heightening one's mental acuity to levels that others who have never experienced such suffering cannot fully comprehend. In suffering, one becomes more aware not only that things are not right within oneself, but perhaps even more those things that are not right in the world. And this is what suffering revealed about Kyle's heart. In other words, Kyle Lovett had a good heart. He wanted things to be better than they are, for him and for others.

While most us were living life in our little bubble, Kyle was seeing and doing things that most young men will never see or be called upon to do. He was keenly aware of many of the absurdities of life. Kyle had an awareness of the world and of the suffering and pain of others that was overwhelming. Folks listen, it's little wonder that he often found relief in alcohol as so many people do. The awareness that things are not as they should be is a heavy burden to carry, especially for a man who wants what is good.

Kyle is not alone in that desire. I am reminded of the words of poet Eve Merriam who penned "I dream of giving birth to a child who will one day ask, 'Mother, what was war?'" How many of us have ever wondered why there is so much pain in the world? How many of us ever questioned God? I know I have. I know Job did in the Old Testament. It was a question that Kyle had too. There were times that Kyle did question the very existence of God. If there is a God, how can there be so much suffering in the world? As Barry said, "Kyle put on a façade that he didn't need God. Because of the pain, he felt great distance from God."

But I also learned that in those times when his inhibitions were lowered by alcohol that he would talk, and as some of us know all too well, in such times we more freely talk about what is really on our hearts and minds. In those times Kyle would talk about God. God was on his heart and mind. Now I will say this, I am not advocating that you bring a keg of beer to your next Bible study, but when the façade is moved out of the way, for every man, the one fundamental question is the existence of God. When Moses was filled with questions, doubts and fears, God himself placed him in the cleft of the mountain and told Moses "There is a place near me where you may stand on a rock." My friends, that rock is Jesus Christ. And the one who longs to know God and find hope ultimately comes face to face with this eternal Rock of Ages.

So, if God is the fundamental question, then as Philosopher, Albert Camus said, "There is only one serious philosophical problem, and that is suicide, deciding whether or not life is worth living." No doubt many of us here today have at some point in our lives had the same thought - Is life worth living? The apostle Paul had a similar thought when he said, "I would much rather go on and be with the Lord, but for your sake I remain."

So, the question on our hearts today: Why did Kyle make the choice he made on Wednesday afternoon? Why will some 40,000 others make the same choice this year across the nation? Friends, I can't give you that answer. But I would say this, that if Kyle could somehow talk to us today from across that great divide, I believe with all my heart that he would tell you that he is sorry. It was not his intention to disappoint you. Lauren, Barry, Cheryl, Zack I believe that he would tell you that he loves you.

Cheryl, you, and I discussed it the other day, and I know that many of you here are aware of the chatter on social media in our community, some of it very negative and hurtful. My encouragement to you and every one of us here today - don't let ignorance rue the day with further pain. This gathering, each one of us can be catalysts for change in our community to help others better understand depression and the impact of traumatic stress and all the subsequent fallout that goes along with it. In his dying, may we be the catalysts for Kyle's dream of a better day becoming a reality in our community and even in the world – a reality where people are more loving and understanding. By our love and compassion and the grace of God may we lessen the suffering of those in pain.

In this time of crisis and loss, may we find one another and realize that we have the freedom to choose life. May the pain that we feel today give us awareness of others who are hurting and in danger, and may we have the boldness and courage to intervene on their behalf. May Kyle's suffering be an opportunity for us to trust once again in a God who loves us and knows that we all see through a glass dimly, we all have questions, but that one day we will see clearly, and we will know even as we are fully known.

As we go from this place today, may we do so with a vision to make Kyle's dream come true of a loving and even less absurd world. Ignorance will not rue the day. Choose rather to focus on the best of the human spirit and the grace of God and his peace that passes all understanding. Even over the past three days I have seen the grace of God and the goodness of the human spirit. I have seen it in a compassionate Police Chief, detectives, and other first responders. I have seen it in a pastor reaching out wanting to know what he can do. I have seen in the response of nearly 1,000 community members in social media responding with understanding, love and prayers and I have seen it in the response of many community members calling wanting to take part in the annual Intervene Challenge here in Fayette County to learn the skills that are saving lives and building stronger community.

To these, I say praise be to God. Kyle's dream of a better day is coming and his memory lives on.

REMEMBERING OTHERS

Dog Tag Dave Remembers Stephanie Hafer
of Clifton Virginia
March 10, 1974 – November 6, 2017

Stephanie touched me in a way that only she could. She was the woman who I was convinced did not exist, the *she* that made this *he* whole again and part of an incredible *we*. I took off my amour and totally exposed my vulnerabilities to her and I☐ was not afraid. Love was our purpose, the price of loving so deeply is the pain of the grief I now feel. But grief cannot erase the beauty that loving her brought to my world. Grief is a small price to pay for the joy that her love printed upon my heart and memory. She will live in my heart forever.

We are adding more Memorials to this section. If you would like to share a fond memory of a loved one of friend that was taken from us to soon, please write to Ken@AFMfamily.com. Memorial should be a maximum of 110 words.

RESOURCES

The following resources are offered as a public service only. We do not run, recommend, endorse, or fund any of the groups listed unless otherwise noted.

1-800-273-TALK (8255) is the number for the National Suicide Prevention Lifeline, a national network of local crisis centers that provides free and confidential emotional support to people in suicidal crisis or emotional distress 24 hours a day, 7 days a week.

Action Alliance for Suicide Prevention is the public-private partnership advancing the National Strategy for Suicide Prevention. The Alliance envisions a nation free from the tragic experience of suicide.

Alliance of Hope provides healing support for people coping with the shock, excruciating grief and complex emotions that accompany the loss of a loved one to suicide. Learn more at AllianceofHope.org.

American Association of Suicidology promotes research, public awareness programs, public education and training for professionals and volunteers. In addition, AAS serves as a national clearinghouse for information on suicide. Learn more at Suicidology.org.

American Foundation for Suicide Prevention raises awareness, funds scientific research, and provides resources and aid to those affected by suicide. Learn more at AFSP.org

Armed Forces Mission founded in 2012 by Army Chaplain Kenneth Koon, AFM is actively engaged in direct intervention of those at risk and the training of others to do the same. Learn more at AFMfamily.org

Healing4Heroes has dual purposes in that it serves the community by helping military personnel and veterans as well as local animal shelters by rescuing suitable dogs. Learn more at Healing4Heroes.org.

Hope and Healing at Hillenglade located in Nashville, provides veterans and their families with a wonderful opportunity to engage with horses and have a fun day unwinding from the stresses of life.

LOSS TEAM Local Outreach to Suicide Survivors is a grassroots movement across the US to train communities on the value of creating LOSS Teams. The goal has been to shorten the elapsed time between the death and survivors finding the help they feel will help them cope with this devastating loss. Learn more at LOSSteam.com

National Alliance on Mental Illness, is the nation's largest grassroots mental health organization dedicated to building better lives for the millions of Americans affected by mental illness. Learn more at NAMI.org.

PTSD PROJECTS seeks to raise awareness and provide general education about the invisible wounds in PTSD. Learn more at PTSDprojects.com.

SAVE is one of the nation's first organizations dedicated to the prevention of suicide. Their work is based on the foundation and belief that suicide is preventable and everyone has a role to play in preventing suicide. Learn more at SAVE.org.

SAVE22 Started out as a US Marine wanting to go on a walk to spread the word and educate people about veteran suicide. It has evolved into a thriving organization making a difference in the lives of America's Veterans. Learn more at SAVE22.vet

Stigmatized: The Suicide Survivor's Journey is a Facebook support group for suicide survivors and those that have been impacted by suicide completion or ideation.

Strategies for Trauma Awareness and Resilience (STAR) STAR is for people whose work brings them in contact with populations dealing with current or historic trauma. Learn more at www.emu.edu/cjp/star/training

STOP SUICIDE USA provides training nationwide in various curriculums. Applied Suicide Intervention Skills Training, Mental Health First Aid, Listen Learn Lead, and others. Stop Suicide is an offshoot of ☐Armed Forces Mission, founded by Kenneth Koon to mirror in the civilian community the success AFM has achieved in the veteran community. Learn more at StopSuicideUSA.org.

The Stronger Alliance is creating a national grassroots movement of like-minded people within communities, churches, workplaces, or schools that stand with our veterans, first-responders, and those affected by traumatic life experiences. Learn more at StrongerAlliance.com

Waypoint Ranch and the Peace at Home Project located in Carrollton, Georgia was founded as a nonprofit organization to provide a place where veteran families can find effective, evidence-based treatments combined with holistic alternative therapies on a working ranch. Learn more at WaypointRanch.org.

RECOMMENDED READING

Healing After Suicide of a Loved One by Ann Smolin, CSW and John Guinan, Ph.D.

Change Your Brain Change your Life by Daniel G. Amen, MD

Cracked, Not Broken by Kevin Hines

Melissa: A Father's Lesson from a Daughter's Suicide by Frank Page

Supernormal: The Untold Story of Adversity and Resilience by Meg Jay, PhD

The Combat Trauma Healing Manual by Chris Adsit

31 Days From Now ~ *Sticking with I DO, Overcoming I'm DONE*, a marriage enrichment book by Kenneth Koon

ABOUT THE AUTHOR

Kenneth Koon is the founder of Armed Forces Mission (AFM) and Stop Suicide USA. AFM is focused primarily on the reduction of suicide within the military, veteran, and first responder communities; while Stop Suicide USA mirrors AFM in the civilian community. Ken returned to service in the US Army Reserve as a chaplain at the age of 45 and currently serves as the Family Life Chaplain for 7,500 soldiers of the 80th Training Command. Ken was honored in 2016 as the Trinity Awards Emergency Responder of the Year and inducted into the University of North Georgia Alumni Hall of Fame in 2018 for his work in suicide intervention. Ken has more than two decades of experience in intervention and emergency response, including service in fire and police departments, military units, hospitals, schools, and the community at large. Ken serves as the on-call Crisis Intervention Team Chaplain for the Peachtree City Police Department. He holds a Master of Divinity in Education and a Doctorate in Pastoral Counseling, and is trained in Clinical Pastoral Education, Crisis Intervention Team (CIT), Community Emergency Response Team (CERT) and Crisis Intervention Stress Management (CISM).

Ken is available for speaking engagements nationwide. Visit ChaplainKen.com to learn more

What Others Say About Listen Learn Lead and the Intervene Challenge

Thousands of caring individuals have taken the Intervene Challenge, gaining the skills to courageously intervene for those at risk. Intervention saves lives! Together we can build a network of care and stop suicide in the USA. Actor Kevin Sorbo

We had an informative and powerful *Listen Learn Lead* seminar to a packed room led by Ken Koon. Our Hillenglade Team is now better prepared to help those who come to us for hope and healing who may be dealing with suicidal thoughts.
Actress Jennifer O'Neill

Because of the efforts of Ken Koon our officers are better equipped to recognize and respond to someone that is considering suicide." Sgt. Brian Eden, Community Outreach Coordinator Peachtree City Police Department

The training was great! Instructors were knowledgeable and personable. Recommend all law enforcement officers take this training. Fantastic job." Lt Josh Duke, Henry County Police Department

We had 13 states represented! It was a great experience and our Buddy Team wants us to do it again! Thank you and your team for taking the time to create this the perfect workshop for us! We look forward to working with you again! Nick and Jan Catinna, PTSD Projects

Excellent workshop! After 40 years in the counseling field, it is rare I say that. Marilyn Roberts, LPC

Rare people who really know how to connect with people... high level of compassion and caring for others. I am grateful to work with such kind and compassionate professionals.
Dr. Paul Wade, Suicide Prevention Program Manager, USAR

A heart for soldiers that extends beyond the Soldiers... Brigadier General John W. Aarsen, USAR

A voice for the needs of soldiers in the civilian community.
Chaplain (COL) Tim Bonner, USAR

A high quality of performance...articulate, caring and sensitive...most commendable. COL. TRACY DAWKINS, USAR

An extraordinary way of reaching people... overwhelmingly touched. Planning the next event now! MAJ Connie Gonzales, Army Suicide Prevention

Chaplain Koon left a legacy in our unit that continues today. Training saves lives and no one I know is more passionate about saving lives and teaching others to do the same than my dear friend and mentor, Chaplain Kenneth Koon. Read the book, gain the skills and you too can turn the tide on suicide in your community. Chaplain (Major) Michael Hildreth, US Army Reserve

Your Financial Support Saves Lives

Suicide is increasing across the US, but intervention saves lives. Your support makes a difference in countless ways.

- $19 a month will provide curriculum for the training of a dozen caregivers annually.
- A one-time gift of $500 will provide curriculum for a workshop of 26 caregivers.

With your support we will train an army of compassionate community members across the nation that have the skills to help those that are at risk. Together we can turn the tide on suicide and build a culture of care and a network of support that strengthens communities, families, and individuals.

Give today…

AFMfamily.org

Armed Forces Mission building resilience and restoring hope for veterans and law enforcement communities

StopSuicideUSA.org

Working in communities nationwide to train people to save people.

We love to collaborate with other organizations in providing workshops for your community. Contact us today.

[i] Lehman, Ellard, and Wortman, 1986. Listening Facts. International Listening Association

[ii] Mehrabian, 1981. Listening Facts. International Listening Association

[iii] Seiden, R. H. (1978), Where Are They Now? A Follow-up Study of Suicide Attempters from the Golden Gate Bridge. Suicide and Life-Threatening Behavior

[iv] Mathias, . C. W., Michael Furr , R., Sheftall, A. H., Hill-Kapturczak, N., Crum, P. and Dougherty, D. M. (2012), Suicide and Life-Threatening Behavior

[v] McGuire-Snieckus R. Hope, optimism, and delusion. *The Psychiatric Bulletin*. 2014.

[vi] Page, Frank, Melissa: A Father's Lesson From a Daughter's Suicide, 2013 B&H Publishing. Nashville

[vii] Archer, Dale MD, The Power of Hope, Psychology Today July 31, 2013

[viii] Sisk, Richard, 'Parking Lot' Suicides Roil VA Hospitals, Military.com August 14, 2017

[ix] Parent, Richard 2004. "Aspects of Police Use of Deadly Force in North America – The Phenomenon of Victim-Precipitated Homicide," Ph.D. thesis, Simon Fraser University.

[x] Riggs, Mike, January 9, 2014 "Think Twice Before Asking the Police to Deal with the Mentally Ill" CITYLAB.com

[xi] Gilbert, Curtis, May 2017 "Not Trained Not to Kill" APMreports.org

[xii] After Suicide: A Toolkit for Schools prepared by the American Foundation for Suicide Prevention and the Suicide Prevention Resource Center

[xiii] Brian L. Mishara, PHD, Marc Daigle, PHD, Cecile Bardon, PHD, Franc Ois Chagnon, PHD, Bogdan Balan, MD, PHD, Sylvaine Raymond, MA, and Julie Campbell, MA, Suicide and Life-Threatening Behavior 46 (5) October 2016 577 published by Wiley Periodicals, Inc. on behalf of American Association of Suicidology

[xiv] Swartz, Aimee, March 17, 2015 Atlantic Press

[xv] Jay, Meg, PhD 2017. "SuperNormal – The Untold Story of Adversity and Resilience" Twelve Books Publishers

[xvi] Amen, Daniel G, MD. 2015. Change Your Brain Change Your Life. Penguin Random House, LLC